Leading Economic Controversies of 1997

Leading Economic Controversies of 1997

EDWIN MANSFIELD
University of Pennsylvania

W. W. Norton & Company
NEW YORK   LONDON

To Beth and Ken

This book is composed in ITC Baskerville
Composition by Com Com
Manufacturing by Haddon
Book design by Martin Lubin

ISBN 0-393-97038-8 (pbk.)
W. W. Norton & Company, Inc.,
500 Fifth Avenue, New York, N.Y. 10110
http://www.wwnorton.com
W. W. Norton & Company Ltd.,
10 Coptic Street, London WC1A 1PU

1 2 3 4 5 6 7 8 9 0

Contents

Preface

E conomics is an exciting subject—or it can be if it is taught properly. Obviously, one of the most important purposes of an elementary economics course is to get students interested in the subject, and this can best be done by showing them how the principles of economics can enable them to understand better the major economic issues of today. That in brief is the purpose of the Third Edition of this book, which focuses on eleven central policy areas: (1) education, (2) the distribution of income, (3) the minimum wage and economic dependency, (4) antitrust policy, (5) the environment, (6) farm policy, (7) GDP and economic growth, (8) fiscal policy, (9) taxation and personal investing, (10) monetary policy, and (11) international trade policy. One-third of the articles included are new to this edition.

These policy areas play a major role in practically any elementary economics course. To arouse students' interest in each of these areas, this book presents contrasting (or in some cases, complementary) views by leading policymakers (like Alan Greenspan, John Kasich, and Daniel Patrick Moynihan), prominent scholars (like Gary Becker, Alan Blinder, David Card and Alan Krueger, Robert Eisner, Robert Hall and Alvin Rabushka, Paul Krugman, Burton Malkiel, and Charles Schultze), and major business executives (like Robert Lutz), as well as government advisory groups like the President's Council of Economic Advisers. Each of the articles is at a level that is appropriate for the typical undergraduate. The articles, many of which are based on speeches, tend to be lighter in tone—and hence more palatable to students—than many other discussions of these issues. Also, it is worth noting that these articles tend to be very up-to-date.

In each of the eleven parts of this book, after the articles presenting different views of a particular issue, there are questions for analysis. These questions, which can form the basis for classroom discussion or homework exercises, are meant to provide an overview of the articles and to encourage the student to relate key points in the articles to the principles of economics.

This book was originally conceived as a supplement to *Economics U.S.A.,* Fourth Edition, but many instructors have used it to supplement other elementary economics textbooks; and some have used it alone.

E.M.

October 1996

PART ONE

EDUCATION

There is general agreement among economists and others
that education is of great importance to the U.S. economy. In
the first article, the Council of Economic Advisers emphasizes
that, "rather than continue to debate how much of a difference [additional resources devoted to education] have made
in the past, we should be asking how programs and incentives
could be structured today to ensure even greater benefits
from resources invested now and in the future." In the next
article, Charles Schultze, senior fellow at the Brookings
Institution, concludes that: "The evidence is overwhelming
that the quality of American elementary and secondary education leaves much to be desired and that the level of American
productivity and living standards has been and will continue
to be lowered by that deterioration in quality."

1

The Payoff to Public Investment in Education*

Joseph Stiglitz

**PRESIDENT CLINTON'S COUNCIL
OF ECONOMIC ADVISERS**

Since the publication of *Equality of Educational Opportunity* (commonly known as the Coleman Report) in 1966, researchers have struggled with the question of whether increased expenditure on schools improves student performance. The debate is often quite contentious because of the large differences in expenditure per pupil between rich and poor school districts. For example, during the 1992–93 school year, New Jersey spent more than $9,400 per pupil in public elementary and secondary schools, while Alabama and Mississippi spent less than $3,900. Regional differences in the cost of living can explain only a small part of such variation. Furthermore, given the importance of local financing of public education, expenditure per pupil can differ by a factor of two or three even between districts in the same State.

Typically, analysts compare average test scores in high-spending and low-spending districts to learn about the effect of additional resources on scores. Not surprisingly, the high-spending districts have higher average scores. However, since high-spending districts also tend to have higher average family income and parental education, the differences in student performance may be caused not by differences in the level of spending but

*This is an excerpt from the *Economic Report of the President* (Washington, D.C.: Government Printing Office, 1996).

by differences in family resources. When analysts compare test scores in high- and low-spending districts with similar family incomes and parental education, the results are often considered provocative: districts that spend more are often found *not* to have higher test scores.

However, additional resources could have other beneficial impacts. The standardized tests used in much of the research may not reliably measure the kinds of improvements that parents or policymakers would expect schools to produce with additional resources. The benefits of new courses in American history, geometry, or calculus or improved learning opportunities for the disabled—valuable as they may be—would not be captured by such measures.

Consistent with this hypothesis, studies of the long-term impacts of school expenditure on earnings and educational attainment—in contrast to those that focus on test scores—yield more optimistic evidence that public investment in elementary and secondary schooling does generate benefits later in students' lives. For instance, better paid and better educated teachers and smaller classroom size have been associated with greater educational attainment and higher payoffs to education later in life, even if they have not had large effects on the particular test scores used. One recent study concluded that the payoff was not only positive but financially lucrative: a 10 percent increase in expenditures from kindergarten through 12th grade would produce additional lifetime earnings valued at 1.2 times the additional cost (in present value terms). Admittedly, studies of this kind remain few, and some authors have reported less positive results, but some evidence suggests that past increases in spending on education did bear fruit, even if the results did not register on the particular tests used.

But the debate over such findings often misses a more relevant question: rather than continue to debate how much of a difference additional resources have made in the past, we should be asking how programs and incentives could be structured today to ensure even greater benefits from resources invested now and in the future. It is difficult to believe that a knowledgeable school principal could not find a way to use additional resources to improve student learning, as long as the incentives in the environment rewarded such gains. The task of policymakers should be to create an environment in which incentives dictate that resources be invested profitably.

On this question, Federal, State, and local governments are already a step ahead of the academic debate. Many of the educational reforms being pursued today seek to produce more decentralization and greater accountability, both of which are designed to create an environment in which resources are used more efficiently. The charter school movement is a good example. Minnesota was the first State to pass a law allowing for charter schools in 1991. Since then 19 other States have enacted laws permitting the development of charter schools. A charter school is usually the brain-child of a committed group of teachers or set of parents who want the flexibility to try a different approach. Typically, they apply to the local school board or the State department of education for a charter allowing them to open a new school with public funding. Since charter schools are public schools, they do not charge tuition. Such charters typically waive many of the regulatory requirements imposed on other public schools for 3 to 5 years, at which time they are subject to review.

Charter schools enhance accountability in two ways. First, charter contracts often specify benchmarks for performance, such as scores on specific state assessments. In exchange for the freedom to innovate, charter school organizers are expected to produce results. Some contracts are more specific in spelling out such performance expectations than others. As states develop better assessment tools under the Goals 2000: Educate America Act, these performance expectations can be more explicitly stated. Second, the presence of charter schools is intended to encourage innovation by nearby public and private schools, through the demonstration of successful educational strategies and through the threat of lost enrollment.

The Department of Education has helped to nurture the charter school movement by providing seed money for the establishment of charter schools. In the 1995 fiscal year, the Federal Government provided nearly $6 million in grants to help cover startup costs for charter schools. The Administration hopes to increase this commitment significantly over the next few years.

But the establishment of charter schools represents only one way in which States and local school districts are seeking to provide better incentives for schools and teachers. School report cards, performance bonuses for schools, magnet schools, and other forms of public school choice are also being tested.

Publicly funded vouchers for use at private schools are another, more radical approach. But vouchers have several problems. Their advocates fail to recognize the many ways in which education for children differs from conventional goods. The primary risk of vouchers is that they may produce a dramatic increase in social stratification. The cost in terms of the resulting damage to social mobility and social cohesion could exceed any benefit in terms of better school performance. Because they are public schools dependent upon public support, charter schools can be more carefully planned to serve all children's interests by locating them in urban areas, by insisting on open admissions policies, by holding them directly accountable for results, and—when oversubscribed—by requiring them to establish lotteries for admission. Charter schools provide a framework for an improved educational system, with parents and teachers working together to develop new and creative solutions to the challenges they face, and demanding accountability of all participants in the educational process.

Some approaches to accountability are better suited to some environments than others. For instance, school report cards are better indicators of school performance when mobility between schools is low and when one can control for differences in student characteristics. Charter schools and magnet schools provide better incentives when the quality of local transportation is good and parents are engaged and well informed. Still another approach, which several European countries employ, raises the stakes for students, through more widespread use of achievement tests as a criterion for high school graduation and college admission, or even by employers in their hiring decisions (Box 1). Given the diversity of circumstances around the country, it is appropriate that each State and school district pursue its own strategy for encouraging more decentralization and accountability.

BOX 1   **RAISING THE STAKES FOR STUDENTS**

Despite recent gains, American youth continue to perform poorly in science and mathematics relative to their counterparts in many other industrialized countries. American students also seem to spend less time on their studies than students in other countries. The Organization for Economic Cooperation and Development has suggested that one of the causes of the poorer U.S. performance is the lack of connection between high school achievement and employment or schooling opportunities.

Unless they are planning to attend a selective college, high school students in America often have little incentive to do well academically. Surveys suggest that employers have difficulty collecting and interpreting transcripts from many different schools. And except for the most competitive colleges, a student's performance in high school has little impact on his or her chances of admission to college. The skills developed in school may well matter later in students' careers, but many students may fail to see a connection between performance in school and immediate prospects for a job or college admission.

In contrast, many European countries require students graduating from high school to take tests in various subject areas. Universities use these scores in making admission decisions, as do employers in their hiring decisions. Some precedent for such high-stakes testing exists in the United States—the Regents Examination in New York is an example. By raising the stakes for high school performance—or, possibly more important, making the actual consequences more visible—these tests may induce students to work harder.

An achievement test may also strengthen the incentives of students and teachers to work together. Absent an external standard, schools judge individual students relative to their classmates. But the relative scale gives students an incentive to discourage their peers from "wrecking the curve." In contrast, an external standard unites teachers, students, and their classmates in a common objective: to perform well.

Education: A Memo to the President*

CHARLES SCHULTZE

T hose who have studied the sources of economic growth agree that increases in the educational qualifications of the American labor force have contributed greatly to the growth in its productivity. The importance of education to productivity growth can also be observed in other countries—the education of a country's work force is an important determinant of its output and income per worker.

THE EDUCATION AND SKILLS OF THE LABOR FORCE

Growth studies rely on the central assumption that economic payoff to education—the higher productivity associated with additional years of education—can be measured by examining the differences in earnings among people with different amounts of education. In the late 1970s, for example, average incomes of full-time (male) workers varied according to years of school completed, as shown in Table 1. The number of years of school completed by American workers has been growing steadily since the country was founded. That growth has continued throughout the postwar period. Using data like that shown in Table 1, Edward Denison

*Charles Schultze is a senior fellow at the Brookings Institution. This article comes from his *Memos to the President* (Washington, D.C.: Brookings, 1992).

TABLE 1 Income Disparity by Years of Schooling

EDUCATION	RATIO
High school dropout	0.84
High school graduate	1.00
1–4 years of college	1.48
5 or more years of college	1.68

found that between 1929 and 1982 the increase in schooling accounted for some 0.4 percent a year of the 1.6 percent annual growth rate in productivity.[1] Moreover, that 0.4 percent a year contribution of education was roughly the same in all the major subperiods, including the years after 1973. The recent productivity slowdown cannot be attributed to a trailing off in the growth of years of schooling among American workers. Other researchers, using more detailed data and some refinements of technique, basically confirm these findings.

The traditional growth studies have relied on data about the quantity of education, as measured by years of school completed. But what about quality? It is widely believed that in recent years the quality of American education has deteriorated. Scores on the Scholastic Aptitude Test (SAT) started a long period of decline after the mid-1960s. Students born in 1945 and tested in 1963 achieved an average score (math plus verbal) of 980. Seventeen years later, in 1980, the cohort of students born in 1962 and tested in 1980 averaged a score of only 890, a 10 percent decline. Could that not be at least one cause of the productivity slowdown?

Most of those who have carefully investigated the question concluded that the decline in educational test scores was unlikely to have been significantly responsible for the slowdown in productivity growth *to date*. It has been estimated that about half of the decline in the SAT scores (and all of the decline before 1973) occurred because an increasing proportion of the high school population was taking them; the tests were reaching further and further down into the ability pool, and quite naturally the average declined. More important, the decline in test scores that began in the late 1960s affected only new entrants to the labor force, and those entrants weren't a large enough proportion of the whole labor force to have been associated with the decline in productivity growth that began occurring in the late 1960s and became worse in the 1970s. Finally, the slowdown in pro-

[1]Edward F. Denison, *Trends in American Economic Growth, 1929–82* (Brookings, 1985), p. 114.

ductivity growth was a worldwide phenomenon and occurred in countries whose educational performance is constantly being held up as examples of success.

Recently, a careful study by John Bishop of Cornell University has suggested that the drop in SAT scores may adversely affect productivity in the future.[2] In the first place, the evidence strongly suggests that prior to the late 1960s the general intellectual achievement of American students, as measured by various tests, had been rising steadily at least since the turn of the century. The evidence also shows that improved intellectual achievement is associated with higher wages and higher productivity. Thus some fraction of the growth in American productivity before 1970 depended on a continuing rise in the quality of education and the intellectual level of the American work force (aside from the improvement simply because of increased years of schooling). To the extent that average test scores measure intellectual achievement—and to a significant extent they do—simply maintaining the earlier (pre-1970s) growth rate of productivity would have required continued improvement in test scores. The decline in scores that occurred after the late 1960s was thus more serious than appears at first glance.

In the decade of the 1970s the downturn in test scores of new entrants to the labor force did not play a large role in the reduction of productivity growth, simply because—as noted above—those young workers formed such a small segment of the overall work force. But, as Bishop warns, the fraction of workers whose test scores fall below the earlier trend is steadily growing as more and more of the work force consists of cohorts of workers who graduated from school after the late 1960s. Even if the recent recovery in test scores continues and represents a real improvement in intellectual achievement, scores will remain for a very long time below the point they would have been had the trends of the 1950s and 1960s been sustained. Thus Bishop calculates that even on the optimistic assumption of continued recovery, the average quality and productivity of the work force in 1990 was 3.6 percent below where earlier trends would have put it, and by the year 2000 the quality shortfall will be 5.5 percent. That's a huge amount. It means a loss of about $250 billion in GNP below its earlier growth path. Although these estimates probably exaggerate the effect of the fall in test scores—it may be unreasonable to have expected the 1950s and 1960s improvements to continue forever—the evidence is strong enough to establish the distinct likelihood that test scores do measure intellectual achievement, even if imperfectly; that improved intellectual achievement

[2]John Bishop, "Is the Test Score Decline Responsible for the Productivity Growth Decline?" *American Economic Review*, vol. 79 (March 1989), pp. 178–97.

of the labor force is associated with productivity growth; and that the post-1960s decline in test scores will be increasingly damping the growth of American productivity, even if some recovery in scores takes place.

BUSINESS PRACTICES AND THE QUALITY OF ELEMENTARY AND SECONDARY EDUCATION

Not only has the apparent intellectual achievement of American high school students declined, but a volume of evidence has accumulated indicating that American elementary and secondary students are not nearly as well prepared as their counterparts in other advanced countries. The American educational system has some advantages over those of many other countries, especially in encouraging independent thinking and innovation. But in imparting knowledge and skills, especially in math and science, American education prepared students far less well than the school systems of many other countries. On standardized tests, American students score much lower than do students of similar age in foreign countries, and the discrepancy seems to grow as the students advance through the elementary and secondary school system. As the most egregious example, the test scores of American students at the end of high school were four grade equivalents behind those of Japanese students with the same number of years in school. But American students at the high school and elementary levels also score poorly compared with students in virtually all other advanced countries. In almost none of the comparisons can the poor U.S. results be explained by the phenomenon that a larger fraction of U.S. students finish high school than is the case in other countries. In a recent report, the National Science Foundation summed up the evidence this way: "Thus, U.S. 10-year-old students in science ranked in the middle of the countries, lost ground by age 14, and scored at or near the bottom by the 12th grade."[3]

There is some reason to believe that those American students who attend college—at least the better four-year colleges—begin to catch up to their foreign counterparts. Certainly competition is intense among foreign students to attend the top American institutions of higher learning. But approximately half of the young people graduating from high school do not go to college; the other half enter the labor force directly from high school.

Over the years, scores of studies have documented the relationship between what a worker scores on tests measuring competence and subsequent productivity in the workplace. Research conducted for the armed

---

[3]National Science Board, *Science and Engineering Indicators—1989* (Washington: Government Printing Office, 1989), p. 28.

forces amply demonstrates the same point. There is clearly a cost to the nation, in forgone productivity and income, that can be associated with the low intellectual achievement of the average American worker who has recently entered the work force after high school.

The same John Bishop cited above has identified at least one potentially removable cause for the poor performance record of American high school students.[4] He assembled a large body of evidence that shows that despite the positive relationship between the productivity of young workers (who have not attended college) and prior educational achievement, there is little connection between the earnings of young male workers during the first five to ten years of work and their educational achievement, and only small gains for young women. For those students not going on to college, there are thus few economic incentives to do well in high school and to score well on performance tests. And, on average, American high school students, not surprisingly, spend a much smaller share of their time in school and are commonly believed to do less homework than their foreign counterparts.

James Rosenbaum of Northwestern University points out that college-bound students have substantial incentives to perform well in high school, and their teachers and administrators have incentives to promote that objective.[5] These incentives are effectively enforced by the colleges who penalize poor work and reward good performance. But for students not aspiring to college, the performance incentives are lacking for student and teacher, because future job and income prospects are not related to school performance. As Rosenbaum notes, a tacit conspiracy exists among students and teachers—if you don't hassle me, I won't hassle you.

Why do employers ignore the positive relationship between prior student achievement and high productivity? Why don't the better students get the better jobs and earn the higher wages? The answers are not entirely clear, but Bishop suggests some probable ones. Although tests are available for measuring performance, though imperfectly, in basic language, math, and other skills, concern over potential racial bias led the Equal Employment Opportunity Commission to issue guidelines in 1971 that led to a sharp decline in the tests' subsequent use by employers. Moreover, unlike the high schools in many other countries, most U.S. high schools do not provide transcripts and teachers' referrals to potential employers. And fi-

---

[4]John Bishop, "Incentives for Learning: Why American High School Students Compare So Poorly to Their Counterparts Overseas," in Commission on Workforce Quality and Labor Market Efficiency, *Investing in People: A Strategy to Address America's Workforce Crisis*, Background Papers, vol. 1 (Department of Labor, 1989).
[5]James E. Rosenbaum, "What If Good Jobs Depended on Good Grades?" *American Educator*, vol. 13 (Winter 1989), pp. 10–15, 40–42.

nally, as Harvard's Richard Murnane suggests, many of the widely used tests do not measure problem solving ability at all well, and problem solving ability is the most important skill in the workplace.[6] Since there is a tendency to teach to tests, students are not well prepared or tested for precisely those traits that will be most useful to them in the workplace.

THE ECONOMIC CONSEQUENCES OF THE EDUCATIONAL SHORTFALL

A sharp increase in the inequality of income has accompanied the slow growth of the American economy since the early 1970s. As we have already seen, after 1973 average family income grew very slowly. Furthermore, the income of the bottom 40 percent of families fell, while income for the top 20 percent, and even more striking, for the top 5 percent, grew handsomely. Perhaps the most important aspect of that rising income inequality is the widening gap between the wages of the college educated and the wages of workers, especially young ones, with a high school or less than high school education. Thus, a recent study by Frank Levy found that in 1986 the average annual earnings of a male, aged twenty-five to thirty-four, with four years of high school were 16 percent lower than they were in 1973 (after adjustment for inflation), while the earnings of the average college graduate were approximately unchanged.[7] Even more dramatically, another study that examined changes in wages for high- and low-paid employees found that by 1990 the wages of the bottom 20 percent of American workers (the lowest paid and presumably the least educated and the least skilled) had fallen some 25 to 30 percent below the point they had been in 1973.[8] Harvard's Richard Freeman and some of his colleagues have estimated that only a modest fraction (20 to 30 percent) of the fall in the relative wages of the less educated took place because of loss of high-paying semiskilled jobs in manufacturing industries such as steel and autos.[9] Rather, it principally reflected an across-the-board decline in wages of the less educated and less skilled in all industries. Moreover, the lower earnings did not reflect a shift in job creation in American industry toward low-skill and away from high-skill jobs. If that had been true, there would have been

[6]Richard J. Murnane, "Education and the Productivity of the Work Force: Looking Ahead," in Robert E. Litan, Robert Z. Lawrence, and Charles L. Schultze, eds., *American Living Standards: Threats and Challenges* (Brookings, 1988), pp. 215–45.
[7]Frank Levy, "Incomes," in Lawrence and Schultze, *American Living Standards,* pp. 108–53.
[8]Chinhui Juhn, Kevin Murphy, and Robert Topel, "Why Has the Natural Rate of Unemployment Increased over Time?" *Brookings Papers on Economic Activity 2:* 1991, pp. 75–133.
[9]McKinley L. Blackburn, David E. Bloom, and Richard B. Freeman, "The Declining Economic Position of Less Skilled American Men," in Gary Burtless, ed., *A Future of Lousy Jobs? The Changing Structure of U.S. Wages* (Brookings, 1990), pp. 31–67.

a surplus of the college educated and a shortage of less well-educated workers, and the relative wages of the college educated population would have been bid down relative to the wages of the high school educated, rather than up as was the case. The problem, in short, is not a scarcity of skilled jobs but a shortage of skilled workers.

It may well be true that no absolute decline has occurred in the educational accomplishments and skills of those entering the labor force out of high school. But as technology advances, American industry and other business firms are increasing the technological sophistication and the skill requirements in the workplace. Unless the average level of skills and problem solving capabilities among the high-school educated work force continually improves, employers are increasingly forced to downgrade the skill content, the productivity, and the wages of many jobs at the lower end of the skill distribution.

The problem of educational quality is made more acute by the increasing globalization of modern production. As transportation costs have fallen around the world, and multinational firms have invested heavily in the rapidly developing countries of the Pacific rim and elsewhere, American workers compete far more often with a worldwide industrial labor force. The old sources of comparative advantage, abundant raw materials and cheap capital, have become much less important, while the human skills of management and workers in mastering high-quality, technologically advanced methods of production, transportation, distribution, and finance have become much more important. Markets for American goods and services produced by skilled, competent, and well-educated workers are expanding rapidly, and international trade is a force boosting the wages of such workers. But correspondingly, American workers with low skills and poor education are increasingly competing with the work force of lower-income but rapidly industrializing countries.

A country whose educational and training institutions continued to improve the skills of one-half of its new labor force entrants (college and post-college graduates) while holding constant the skills of the remainder would experience a growing maldistribution of income in the absence of any world trade. But that result will be even more striking as economic and technological developments internationalize world markets. This wave of developments will not recede. Improved education and skill training, not protection, is the answer.

POLICY RESPONSES

The evidence is overwhelming that the quality of American elementary and secondary education leaves much to be desired and that the level of American productivity and living standards has been and will continue to be lowered by that deterioration in quality. The discipline of economics does not offer specific proposals to deal with this problem. But it can provide a few tips. In particular, economics stresses the importance of incentives.

Incentives for Students

John Bishop, correctly I think, has put his finger on one serious problem and pointed in the general direction of what might be done to improve the situation. Employers should be able to reward previous achievement at the high school level by assigning jobs and wage levels on the basis of that performance as indicated by grades and achievement test results, in turn creating some incentives, which apparently do not now exist, for young people to do better in high school even when they are not going on to college. The federal government could sponsor the research and validation needed to improve existing tests, or design and validate new ones, that better measure future performance for white and minority youth. Emphasis should be on testing for problem solving skills. In a related vein, those states that do not have standardized statewide tests should adopt the requirement that all schools administer them. With the states, the federal government could help develop the institutional framework and the privacy protection that would make it feasible for employers, even small- and medium-sized ones, to request and receive in timely fashion high school grades and standardized test scores from high schools, for job applicants (with, of course, the consent of the applicant).

Incentives for Schools

Better incentives in the form of a future wage payoff from good performance should motivate students to put forth more effort. Schools and teachers also need better incentives. It is not the province of economics to design incentives for educational institutions. Nevertheless, the logic of economics would generally favor suggestions, which have been put forward recently, urging the decentralization of local systems, eliminating large slices of central educational bureaucracies, giving more power to principals and teachers in individual schools, and in particular providing parents with the right of choice among individual schools.[10] While the analogy with the marketplace is far from perfect and should not be pushed to the limit, economic history and analysis strongly confirm the benefits for consumers of having vigorous competition among the providers of consumer services

---

[10]See John E. Chubb and Terry M. Moe, *Politics, Markets, and America's Schools* (Brookings, 1990).

and can attest to the spur to performance imparted by the threat of loss of markets.

Finally, in considering these matters, one must bear in mind the simple arithmetic of schools and labor markets. Realistically, better incentives for students and schools and other improvements in educational quality would only begin to affect the performance of high school graduates some years down the pike. In turn, each year's cohort of new workers represents only about 2 to 3 percent of the total labor force. Thus, even educational improvements set in motion immediately would not reach half of the labor force until after the year 2020. And so we should consider means to upgrade the skills of today's adult workers. In the end, hard-headed analysis may indicate little promise for a large-scale effort to educate adult workers. But it would be a mistake to neglect this possibility in the absence of such a negative finding.

QUESTIONS FOR ANALYSIS

1. How much difference do additional resources have on test scores?

2. What are the advantages of charter schools?

3. Do you favor publicly funded vouchers for use at private schools? Why or why not?

4. If they are not planning to attend a selective college, do high school students have much incentive to do well academically?

5. Is there evidence that the quality of U.S. education has deteriorated in recent years?

6. Are U.S. elementary and secondary students as well prepared as their counterparts in other countries?

7. As technology advances, U.S. industry is increasing the technological sophistication and the skill requirements in the workplace. If the average level of skill among the high-school-educated workforce does not improve, what will happen to the wages of many jobs at the lower end of the skill distribution?

8. What role do incentives play? How can they be improved?

PART TWO

THE

DISTRIBUTION

OF INCOME

Two of the big concerns of the mid-1990s have been the relatively slow rate of growth of real income in the United States and the growing inequality of incomes, but there has been considerable debate about what these trends mean and don't mean. The first article, by President Clinton's Council of Economic Advisers, attributes the slow growth of real income to a slowdown in productivity growth and the increase in inequality to increasing returns to education and experience. The second article, by the Republican members of the Joint Economic Committee of Congress, attacks some of the statistical evidence used to support the proposition that income inequality has increased.

Slowing Wage Growth and Widening Inequality*

Laura D'Andrea Tyson

PRESIDENT CLINTON'S COUNCIL OF ECONOMIC ADVISERS*

In the last two decades, family income growth has stagnated and incomes have become more unequally distributed. In fact, the real incomes of the bottom 60 percent of American families were lower in the early 1990s than for the analogous families at the end of the 1970s. Underlying the rising disparity in the fortunes of American families has been a rise in labor market inequality that has shifted wage and employment opportunities in favor of the more educated and the more experienced. Less educated workers suffered substantial losses in real earnings during the 1980s. Here we consider the dimensions, and some likely causes, of slow income growth and widening inequality.

SLOW INCOME GROWTH

Income trends have been discouraging for about two decades—the median family today has virtually the same real income as the median family 20

*This is an excerpt from the *Economic Report of the President* (Washington, DC: Government Printing Office, 1994).

19

CHART 1 Real Hourly Compensation and Wages

The growth of real compensation per hour and of real hourly wages has declined since 1973.

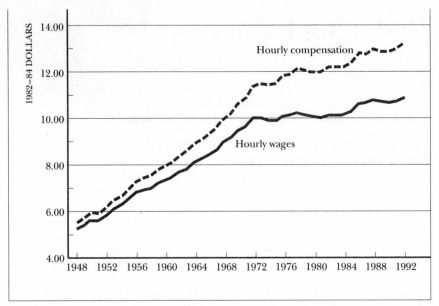

Note: Compensation and average hourly earnings deflated by CPI-U-X1.
Sources: Department of Commerce and Department of Labor.

years ago. This stagnation is a marked departure from the substantial income growth that occurred over previous generations.

From 1947 to 1973 the real income of the median American family increased by a robust 2.8 percent a year, more than doubling. In contrast, from 1973 to 1992 the income of the typical American family was essentially stagnant, rising by only 0.1 percent a year after adjusting for inflation. (The trend from 1979 to 1989—roughly equivalent years in the economic cycle—is similar.) At the pace of income growth from 1973 to 1992, it would take centuries for real median family income to double.

Although the labor force participation decisions of women and changes in the composition of families have affected family income, the major trends in family income are dominated by trends in real wages. Chart 1 shows the changes in wages and total hourly compensation, adjusted for inflation, since 1948. Both wages and compensation suffered abrupt slowdowns in growth rates around 1973.

BOX 1   **GROWING INEQUALITY OF EMPLOYMENT AND UNEMPLOYMENT**

The falling relative wages of those with less experience and schooling may explain, at least in part, some of the observed changes in employment-to-population ratios for certain demographic groups. The black and teenage populations tend to have less schooling than the average for all Americans. Consequently, the wages they command have fallen, making work less attractive. To the extent that the shift in demand away from less-educated workers is manifest in fewer available jobs instead of lower wages, these groups face higher unemployment rates as well.

GROWING INEQUALITY

Families have been affected unevenly by recent income trends. Real incomes at the top have increased smartly, real incomes at the middle have essentially stagnated, and real incomes at the bottom have fallen. Box 1 discusses the implications of these developments for employment and unemployment.

From 1973 to 1992, the average real income of the upper 20 percent of families rose 19 percent, or about 1 percent per year. This is well below the rate for the 1950s and 1960s, but far better than for the rest of the population. Between 1973 and 1992, the average income of the middle 20 percent of families rose a paltry 4 percent in real terms. Lower income families fared even worse. Among the bottom 20 percent of families, mean real income fell by 12 percent from 1973 to 1992. Chart 2 shows the growth of mean family incomes for different income groups over the periods before and after 1973. It makes clear just how abrupt the changes in the distribution of income growth have been. A trend toward greater equality in the 1960s and toward greater inequality in the 1970s and 1980s is apparent in both income and consumption measures of economic well-being. Rising inequality of family incomes during the 1980s is apparent in both pretax and posttax income measures.

EXPLAINING SLOW WAGE GROWTH

Stagnant wages and slow total compensation growth since the early 1970s largely reflect a substantial slowdown in productivity growth. [Productivity is defined as output per hour of labor.] From 1947 to 1973 productivity rose at a compound annual rate of 3.1 percent, and inflation-adjusted compensation per hour grew at a similar rate. From 1973 to 1979 the rate of productivity growth fell to an average of 0.8 percent a year, and compensation growth fell with it. Since 1979 the productivity growth rate has picked

CHART 2 Average Annual Growth of Mean Family Income by Income Quintile

Family incomes in all income groups grew more or less evenly, but slightly faster for lower income groups, before 1973.

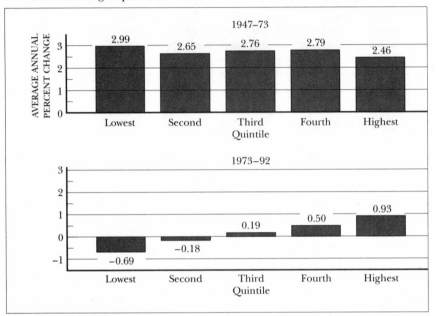

Source: Department of Commerce.

up only slightly, averaging 1.2 percent on an annual basis. [There is a] close relation between productivity and real compensation. Boxes 2 and 3 discuss some of the other effects of productivity growth.

The productivity slowdown has been intensely studied. Many partial explanations have been given, but no complete accounting has been made.

EXPLAINING THE GROWTH OF INEQUALITY

Several factors have contributed to widening inequality. One major factor is increasing returns to education and experience. The college–high school wage premium increased by over 100 percent for workers aged 25 to 34 between 1974 and 1992, while increasing 20 percent for all workers 18 years old and over. In addition, among workers without college degrees, the average wages of older workers increased relative to those of younger workers. Since the relative supply of educated workers has increased at the same time that wage disparities have grown, the demand for educated workers must have increased faster than their supply. Some have suggested

CHART 3 Productivity Growth and Price Reductions, 1950–90

Productivity growth in an industry leads to lower relative prices.

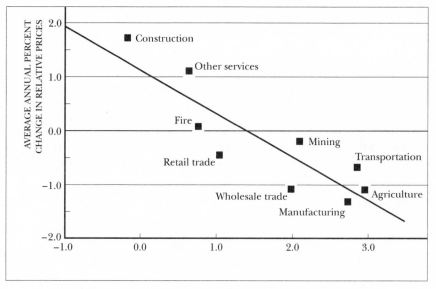

AVERAGE ANNUAL PERCENT CHANGE IN PRODUCTIVITY

Note: FIRE = finance, insurance, and real estate.

Source: Department of Commerce.

BOX 2 CONSEQUENCES OF PRODUCTIVITY GROWTH

Rising productivity has been shown to have a variety of beneficial effects:

□ *The prices of goods produced by industries that have had rapid productivity growth have fallen relative to those of goods from industries with slower productivity growth.* Chart 3 shows average productivity growth and price changes by industry for the 1950–90 period.

□ *Periods of rapid productivity growth have been accompanied by increases in real wages.* The prices of products in industries experiencing productivity growth also decline relative to wages. This decline in product prices means that real wages tend to rise during periods of rapid productivity growth.

□ *Periods of rapid productivity growth have also been periods of low inflation.* Productivity growth allows nominal wages to increase without putting pressure on prices.

□ *Periods of rapid productivity growth have not been associated with large increases in unemployment.* In periods when productivity growth was more rapid, such as the 1960s, unemployment rates have tended to be low. In contrast, periods with slow rates of productivity growth, such as the 1970s, have been periods of relatively high unemployment.

BOX 3   WHY PRODUCTIVITY GROWTH DOES NOT CAUSE UNEMPLOYMENT

Productivity growth need not cause an increase in unemployment because, as productivity rises, more goods can be produced with the same number of workers.
This means a cost saving, which must result in either increased profits, increased
wages, or lower prices. If profits or wages increase, those benefiting from the
increase will increase their spending. If prices fall, consumers' incomes will go
further and they will buy more. In any case, the increased spending will lead to
the purchase of more goods and services, which will create new jobs offsetting
losses from the productivity increase. If the new jobs created are not equal in
number to the jobs lost, there will be a tendency for wages to change to equate
supply and demand for labor. Nonetheless, in the short run some workers are
likely to have to change jobs. As the discussion of the costs of job loss makes clear,
this can be a traumatic experience for the established worker.

---

that increasing trade has undermined demand for less-educated workers in
the United States, since they are plentiful elsewhere in the world. So far,
however, several studies have been unable to discern any substantial impact
of trade on wage inequality, however. If increased trade were the cause of
growing wage inequality, the relative prices of goods that use highly educated labor would be rising relative to those of goods that use less highly educated labor. But studies have found no evidence of such a change in
relative prices. Similarly, if increased trade were responsible for increased
wage inequality, the growth of wage differentials would lead firms in all sectors to substitute less-educated labor for more-educated labor. Instead,
studies find that virtually all manufacturing industries have increased their
relative use of educated labor despite growing wage differentials. Rising
wage differentials with greater use of educated labor suggest that demand
for skilled labor has been rising broadly in the economy. Thus it appears
that most of the demand shift toward highly educated workers must have
originated domestically.

Since the use of more-educated labor has increased in all industries, a
logical explanation of this trend is technical change. For example, one
study shows that people who work with personal computers earn a substantial wage premium over those who do not, and that this can account for
half of the increasing gap between the wages of college and high school
graduates.

Although changes in labor demand induced by changes in the composition of trade do not appear to explain much of the increase in income inequality, the internationalization of the U.S. economy may affect wages in
other ways. For example, the threat of increased import competition or of

the relocation of a factory to another country may undermine worker bargaining power or cause a decline in the number of workers employed in unionized firms. At this time, no reliable studies have properly quantified how important such effects have been. In addition, there is no guarantee that the future will resemble the past. Trade could become a more important factor in bringing down the wages of less-educated workers in the future. On the other hand, technical change could move in the direction of economizing on educated labor and making better use of less-educated labor.

In addition to rapidly increasing demand for educated labor, two institutional factors seem to have contributed to rising wage inequality: the decline of unions and the erosion of the minimum wage by inflation. In the early 1970s, 27 percent of the work force were union members. By 1990 that fraction had declined to 16 percent, and it has probably fallen further since. Several studies conclude that this decline can account for about 20 percent of the increase in wage inequality.

In 1970 the minimum wage was 50 percent of the average hourly wage of private production and nonsupervisory workers. By 1992 it had fallen to 40 percent of the average. This erosion of the minimum wage has allowed a substantial fattening of the lower tail of the wage distribution and contributed to increasing wage inequality. The effect of the minimum wage on the distribution of income is less obvious, since it is possible that the decline in the inflation-adjusted minimum wage may have caused an increase in employment of low-wage workers.

Immigration has increased the relative supply of less-educated labor and appears to have contributed to the increasing inequality of income, but the effect has been small. A study of the effects of immigration between 1980 and 1988 found that it explains less than 1 percent of the change in the college–high school wage differential. Although immigration flows were considerably larger in the late 1980s than the early 1980s, this study makes it seem unlikely that immigration could explain more than a few percent of the total change in this differential.

Chris Frenze

Income Mobility and Economic Opportunity*

JOINT ECONOMIC COMMITTEE OF CONGRESS: REPUBLICAN VIEWS

G reat attention has been given to changes over time in the average incomes of "quintiles," families or households ranked top to bottom by income and divided into fifths. However, such time-line comparisons between rich and poor ignore a central element of the U.S. economy, which is the extent to which individuals move from one quintile to another. Figures on income mobility are more characteristic of the nature of our fluid society than comparisons of average incomes by quintile, which would only be statistically meaningful if America were a caste society where the people comprising the quintiles remained constant over time.

Unfortunately, while data on average income by quintile has been plentiful, however misleading, data on income mobility has been scarce.

This section, an analysis of data based on income tax returns filed from 1979 through 1988, which were tabulated by the U.S. Department of the Treasury, provides new insights. The Treasury sample consists of 14,351 taxpayers filing returns in all of the above years. This sample tends to understate income mobility to the extent the movement of younger and older filers in and out of the population of taxpayers is missed by the requirement that returns be filed in all years. On the other hand, this understate-

*Joint Economic Committee of Congress, *1993 Joint Economic Report*, April 1, 1993.

ment is at least somewhat offset at the low end of the income scale by the presence of an underclass which does not file tax returns year after year. For our purposes, the bottom quintile consists of those who earn enough income to at least file income tax returns, if not to actually pay taxes.

Earlier studies of income mobility have demonstrated a startling degree of income mobility in as short a period as one year. However, as a January 1992 study noted,[1] additional data over more extended periods were needed to draw more precise conclusions about income mobility over the longer term. This need has now been largely satisfied by the provision of longitudinal panel data from tax return files. However, much more data and research on income dynamics in coming years is needed.

LEVEL OF INCOME MOBILITY BY QUINTILE

The tax return data support the conclusion that the degree of income mobility in American society renders the comparison of quintile income levels over time virtually meaningless. According to the tax data, 85.8 percent of filers in the bottom quintile in 1979 had exited this quintile by 1988. The corresponding mobility rates were 71 percent for the second lowest quintile, 67 percent for the middle quintile, 62.5 percent for the fourth quintile, and 35.3 percent for the top quintile.

Of those in the much discussed top 1 percent, over half, or 52.7 percent, were gone by 1988. These data understate income mobility in the top 1 percent to the extent mortality contributes to mobility and the diffusion of income. Chart 1 displays the income mobility of the various groups.

In all but the top quintile, at least 60 percent of filers exited their 1979 income quintile by 1988, with two-thirds or more exiting in the bottom three quintiles. Though much more stability was observed in the top fifth, over one-third had slipped downward to be replaced by others moving up. Even most of the top 1 percent had exited by 1988, to be replaced by others.

The very high degree of income mobility displayed above shows that the composition of the various quintiles changes greatly over time. A majority of filers have indeed moved to different quintiles between 1979 and 1988. Thus intertemporal comparisons of average wages, earnings, or private incomes of quintiles cannot provide meaningful measures of changes in the income of actual families and persons only temporarily in a given quintile or percentile. Quintiles may be a convenient way of presenting snapshots of income data for a group of people at a certain point in time. Nonethe-

[1] JEC/GOP staff study, "Income Mobility and the U.S. Economy: Open Society or Caste System?" released by Congressman Dick Armey, January 1992.

CHART 1   Proportion Moving to Different Quintiles or from Top
Percentile, 1979–88

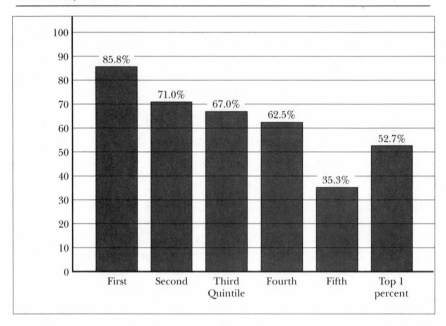

Source: United States Treasury.

less, the notion of a quintile as a fixed economic class or social reality is a
statistical mirage.

DIRECTION OF INCOME MOBILITY

Movement is important, but the direction of that movement is more important. While a strong argument can be made for a flexible and open market economy which presents opportunities to lower and middle income
workers, instability alone is not necessarily a virtue. [Table 1] summarizes
the income mobility data to display the direction of movement between
1979 and 1988. For example, in the third, or middle 1979 fifth, 47.3 percent had moved to a higher quintile by 1988, while 33.0 remained in this
same quintile, and 19.7 percent fell into a lower quintile.

  Given the relative starting position, the very high mobility from the bottom quintile obviously reflects improvement. In addition, the upward
movement in the second, third, and fourth quintiles is much larger than

TABLE 1   America on the Move

1979 QUINTILE	PERCENT IN QUINTILE IN 1979	PERCENT IN EACH QUINTILE IN 1988				
		1ST	2ND	3RD	4TH	5TH
1st	100%	14.2%	20.7%	25.0%	25.3%	14.7%
2nd	100	10.9	29.0	29.6	19.5	11.1
3rd	100	5.7	14.0	33.0	32.3	15.0
4th	100	3.1	9.3	14.8	37.5	35.4
5th	100	1.1	4.4	9.4	20.3	64.7

Source: United States Treasury.

downward movement. For example, 60 percent of the second quintile had moved to one of the higher three quintiles by 1988. Over this same time, only 10.9 percent had fallen from the second into the lowest quintile.

In the long-overdue debate over the significance of income mobility, some may argue that mobility would tend to reflect slippage, especially among the middle class. The data contradict this contention. Of those in the middle quintile in 1979, nearly half moved upward to the fourth or fifth quintiles by 1988. Overall, in the bottom four quintiles, net improvement was the rule, not the exception.

DETAIL ON INCOME MOBILITY, 1979–88

Table 1 displays the movement of filers from 1979 quintiles to their positions in 1988. Each row can be read across: of 100 percent of each 1979 quintile, the table shows their dispersion among the various fifths by 1988.

About 86 percent of those in the bottom quintile in 1979 had managed to raise their incomes by 1988 enough to have moved up to a higher quintile. The data show that these were not all grouped at the bottom at the second quintile. While 20.7 percent were in the second quintile, 25.0 percent had made it into the middle fifth, and another 25.3 percent into the second highest quintile. The 14.7 percent in the top quintile was actually higher than the 14.2 percent still stuck in the bottom fifth.

In other words, a member of the bottom income bracket in 1979 would have a better chance of moving to the top income bracket by 1988 than remaining in the bottom bracket.

In the second quintile, 71 percent had exited between 1979 and 1988. Though 29.0 percent still remained in the second quintile in 1988, 29.6

percent had moved up to the third quintile, 19.5 percent to the fourth, and 11.1 percent to the top quintile. Only 10.9 percent had moved down to the lowest quintile.

Of those in the middle quintile in 1979, 32.3 percent had moved to the fourth quintile and 15.0 percent to the fifth quintile by 1988.

Over this period, 47.3 percent had moved up, while 19.7 percent had moved down. The net effect of income mobility in the middle range clearly reflected net overall improvement.

While the fourth quintile exhibited powerful income mobility, the top quintile is the most stable. However, all income mobility from the top quintile is by definition downward mobility. The share of this group dropping into lower quintiles was 35.3 percent, while 27.2 percent of the fourth quintile also dropped at least one quintile. Many of these with declining fortunes are still better off than many of those with upward mobility from a low quintile, however, the overall pattern is that there tends to be strong upward mobility from the lower quintiles, while income mobility from a high level often reflects economic reversals. Without income mobility, many in the top fifth would be better off, and the great majority of those in the lower quintiles would be worse off. Income mobility reflects improvement in the lower four quintiles, but this fact has been virtually ignored in public discussion of income trends.

While 35.3 percent fell from the top quintile into the fourth quintile or below, 40.0 percent of the bottom quintile had moved into the fourth or fifth quintiles by 1988. Of all of those in the bottom quintile in 1979, about two-thirds, or 65 percent, had moved to the middle or higher quintiles by 1988. These data demonstrate that the U.S. economy, not without problems over this period, still remains dynamic, open, and productive enough to permit most Americans in the bottom three-fifths to work their way up the economic ladder. What is needed are policies to ensure that this flexibility and opportunity are extended as widely as possible, especially to those who actually fall below the bottom fifth of taxpayers.

Currently there are two models of the American economy, one static, and the other dynamic. The first portrays the United States as a caste system and misapplies the characteristics of a permanent income strata to those only temporarily moving through income brackets. The alternative view portrays a much more complex and interesting social reality in which the composition of income classes are in constant flux. According to this latter point of view, simplistic generalizations about actual persons and families (or "the rich" and "the poor") cannot be drawn from data on a conceptual artifice that does not exist as such in reality.

The empirical data support the view of the market economy as a dynamic and open society that provides opportunity to those who participate. There is no evidence of stagnation, with the turnover rate in the most stable quintile—the top fifth—exceeding 35 percent. The turnover rates in the bottom four quintiles were at least 60 percent over the period, with most of this reflecting upward progress. Analysis that assumes or suggests stable composition of family or household income quintiles rests on invalid assumptions.

It makes no sense to draw sweeping conclusions such as "the income of the bottom 20 percent of families fell" in a 15-year period when most of the people originally in that category have long since improved their standard of living enough to have moved up from the bracket entirely.

QUESTIONS FOR ANALYSIS

1. What are the effects of productivity growth? Does productivity growth have to cause unemployment? Why or why not?

2. Are there any reasons why we should be concerned about increases or decreases in income inequality? If so, what are they?

3. According to President Clinton's Council of Economic Advisers, "Stagnant wages and slow total compensation growth since the early 1970s largely reflect a substantial slowdown in productivity growth." Why would a slowdown in productivity growth be expected to have this effect? Explain.

4. President Clinton's Council of Economic Advisers concludes that: "Rising wage differentials with greater use of educated labor suggest that demand for skilled labor has been rising broadly in the economy." Can you show that this is the case, using demand and supply curves for educated labor?

5. Other factors cited by President Clinton's Council of Economic Advisers as possible reasons for growing wage inequality are "the decline of unions and the erosion of the minimum wage by inflation." Are increases in *wage* inequality the same thing as increases in *income* inequality? Why or why not? Is it possible that a big hike in the minimum wage might raise, not lower, income inequality? Why or why not?

6. According to the Republican members of Congress's Joint Economic Committee, "Great attention has been given to changes over time in the average incomes of 'quintiles,' families or households ranked top to bottom by income and divided into fifths. However, such time-line comparisons between rich and poor ignore a central element of the U.S. economy, which is the extent to which individuals move from one quintile to another." Do you agree that such movement is important? Why or why not?

7. The Republican members of the Joint Economic Committee state that: "The empirical data support the view of the market economy as a dynamic and open society that provides opportunity to those who participate." Do you agree? Why or why not?

8. Do you agree with the following conclusion: "It makes no sense to draw sweeping conclusions such as 'the income of the bottom 20 percent of families fell' in a 15-year period when most of the people originally in that category have long since improved their standard of living enough to have moved up from the bracket entirely." Why do you agree or disagree?

PART THREE

THE MINIMUM WAGE AND ECONOMIC DEPENDENCY

Related to the debate over inequality of incomes has been a continuing debate over the minimum wage. Whereas the traditional view in economics has been that an increase in the minimum wage reduces employment, David Card and Alan Krueger of Princeton University have challenged this view. The *New York Times,* in an editorial, argues that the employment effects of an increase in the minimum wage would be small, and that such an increase "would be a victory for public policy." In contrast, Gary Becker of the University of Chicago believes that: "The Card-Krueger studies are flawed and cannot justify going against the accumulated evidence from the many past and present studies that find sizable negative effects of higher minimums on employment." The final article in this section, by Senator Daniel Patrick Moynihan (D., N.Y.), argues that destitution in childhood, relatively independent of economic forces, has become our principal social problem.

A Challenge to the Traditional View*

David Card

Alan Krueger

DAVID CARD AND ALAN KRUEGER

Nearly 50 years ago, George Stigler implored economists to be "outspoken, and singularly agreed" that increases in the minimum wage reduce employment. The reasoning behind this prediction is simple and compelling. According to the model presented in nearly every introductory economics textbook, an increase in the minimum wage lowers the employment of minimum-wage workers. This logic has convinced most economists: polls show that more than 90 percent of professional economists agree with the prediction that a higher minimum wage reduces employment. Such a high degree of consensus is remarkable in a profession renowned for its bitter disagreements. But there is one problem: *the evidence is not singularly agreed that increases in the minimum wage reduce employment.* [We] present a new body of evidence showing that recent minimum-wage increases have not had the negative employment effects predicted by the textbook model. Some of the new evidence points toward a *positive* effect of the minimum wage on employment; most shows no effect at all. Moreover, a reanalysis of previous minimum-wage studies finds little support for the prediction that minimum wages reduce employment. If accepted, our findings call into question the standard model of the labor

*This is an excerpt from David Card and Alan Krueger, *Myth and Measurement* (Princeton, N.J.: Princeton University Press, 1995). Professors Card and Krueger are at Princeton University.

market that has dominated economists' thinking for the past half century.

Our main empirical findings can be summarized as follows. First, a study of employment in the fast-food industry after the recent 1992 increase in the New Jersey minimum wage shows that employment was *not* affected adversely by the law. Our results are derived from a specially designed survey of more than 400 restaurants throughout New Jersey and eastern Pennsylvania, conducted before and after the increase in the New Jersey minimum wage. Relative to restaurants in Pennsylvania, where the minimum wage remained unchanged, we find that employment in New Jersey actually *expanded* with the increase in the minimum wage. Furthermore, when we examine restaurants within New Jersey, we find that employment growth was *higher* at restaurants that were forced to increase their wages to comply with the law than at those stores that already were paying more than the new minimum. We find similar results in studies of fast-food restaurants in Texas after the 1991 increase in the federal minimum wage, and of teenage workers after the 1988 increase in California's minimum wage.

Second, a cross-state analysis finds that the 1990 and 1991 increases in the federal minimum wage did not affect teenage employment adversely. The federal minimum increased from $3.35 per hour to $3.80 on April 1, 1990, and to $4.25 per hour on April 1, 1991. We categorized states into groups on the basis of the fraction of teenage workers who were earning between $3.35 and $3.80 per hour just before the first minimum-wage increase took effect. In high-wage states, such as California and Massachusetts, relatively few teenagers were in the range in which the minimum-wage increase would affect pay rates, whereas in low-wage states, such as Mississippi and Alabama, as many as 50 percent of teenagers were in the affected wage range. On the basis of the textbook model of the minimum wage, one would expect teenage employment to decrease in the low-wage states, where the federal minimum wage raised pay rates, relative to high-wage states, where the minimum had far less effect. Contrary to this expectation, our results show no meaningful difference in employment growth between high-wage and low-wage states. If anything, the states with the largest fraction of workers affected by the minimum wage had the largest gains in teenage employment. This conclusion continues to hold when we adjust for differences in regional economic growth that occurred during the early 1990s, and conduct the analysis with state-level data, rather than regional data. A similar analysis of employment trends for a broader sample of low-wage workers, and for employees in the retail trade and restaurant industries, likewise fails to uncover a negative employment effect of the federal minimum wage.

Third, we update and reevaluate the time-series analysis of teenage employment that is the most widely cited evidence for the prediction that a higher minimum wage reduces employment. When the same econometric specifications that were used during the 1970s are re-estimated with data from more recent years, the historical relationship between minimum wages and teenage employment is weaker and no longer statistically significant. We also discuss and reanalyze several previous minimum-wage studies that used cross-sectional or panel data. We find that the evidence showing the minimum wage has no effect or a positive effect on employment is at least as compelling as the evidence showing it has an adverse effect.

Fourth, we document a series of anomalies associated with the low-wage labor market and the minimum wage. An increase in the minimum wage leads to a situation in which workers who previously were paid different wages all receive the new minimum wage. This finding is difficult to reconcile with the view that each worker originally was paid exactly what he or she was worth. Increases in the minimum wage also generate a "ripple effect," leading to pay raises for workers who previously earned wages above the new minimum. More surprisingly, increases in the minimum wage do not appear to be offset by reductions in fringe benefits. Furthermore, employers have been reluctant to use the subminimum-wage provisions of recent legislation. Each of these findings casts further doubt on the validity of the textbook model of the minimum wage.

Fifth, we find that recent increases in the minimum wage have reduced wage dispersion, partially reversing the trend toward rising wage inequality that has dominated the labor market since the early 1980s. Contrary to popular stereotypes, minimum-wage increases accrue disproportionately to individuals in low-income families. Indeed, two-thirds of minimum-wage earners are adults, and the earnings of a typical minimum-wage worker account for about one-half of his or her family's total earnings. In states in which the recent increases in the federal minimum wage had the greatest impact on wages, we find that earnings increased for families at the bottom of the earnings distribution. The minimum wage is a blunt instrument for reducing overall poverty, however, because many minimum-wage earners are not in poverty, and because many of those in poverty are not connected to the labor market. We calculate that the 90-cent increase in the minimum wage between 1989 and 1991 transferred roughly $5.5 billion to low-wage workers (or 0.2 percent of economy-wide earnings)—an amount that is smaller than most other federal antipoverty programs, and that can have only limited effects on the overall income distribution.

Sixth, we examine the impact of news about minimum-wage legislation on the value of firms that employ minimum-wage workers. Stock market event studies suggest that most of the news about the impending minimum-wage increases during the late 1980s led to little or no change in the market value of low-wage employers, such as restaurants, hotels, and dry cleaners. In contrast, more recent news of possible increases in the minimum wage may have led to small declines in shareholder wealth—1 or 2 percent, at most.

If a single study found anomalous evidence on the employment effect of the minimum wage, it could be easily dismissed. But the broad array of evidence presented in this book is more difficult to dismiss. Taken as a whole, our findings pose a serious challenge to the simple textbook theory that economists have used to describe the effect of the minimum wage.

Boost the
Minimum Wage*

NEW YORK TIMES

There is a strong case for raising the minimum wage by a modest amount. Unfortunately, the issue is caught up in election-year politics, making compromise unlikely. Senate Democrats rounded up 55 members last week to force a vote on it, but they needed 60 votes so the effort failed. Few Democrats shed tears, since they could pin the defeat on the majority leader, Bob Dole.

The Democrats proposed raising the minimum wage over two years to $5.15 an hour, which would raise earnings for these workers by 90 cents an hour, or about $1,800 a year. Even at $5.15, the minimum wage would, after taking account of inflation, remain 15 percent below its average value during the 1970's.

Will low-paid workers lose their jobs if employers must pay higher wages? Yes, but there is widespread agreement among economic studies that the impact would be very small. A 90-cent wage hike would probably wipe out fewer than 100,000 of the approximately 14 million low-paid jobs in the economy—less than a 1 percent loss. Indeed, 100,000 represents only about half the number of jobs the economy typically creates each *month*.

The benefits of a higher minimum wage would be substantial. At $4.25 an hour, minimum-wage workers cannot count on earning their way out of

*This editorial appeared in the *New York Times* on April 5, 1996.

poverty. But at $5.15 an hour, or $10,700 a year, the goal is in reach. By combining earnings, food stamps worth about $3,000 and tax credits of $3,500, such workers can clear the poverty threshold for a family of four—about $16,000—even after payroll taxes. That would be a victory for public policy.

The Republicans criticize the minimum wage as a crude antipoverty tool, and in a sense they are right. For one thing, about 40 percent of the recipients are teen-agers, some from middle-class families. A better tool, which enjoys bipartisan support is the earned income tax credit. The tax credit directly benefits low-paid workers, either by cutting their taxes or, if they owe no tax, giving them a check from the Treasury. The credit is structured to encourage the poor to go to work without hitting their employers.

There are, however, limits to how much higher Congress can push the tax credit. Congress sets the credit for poor workers, and phases it out as wages rise. The higher the initial credit is, the faster the phaseout must become in order to limit the impact of the tax credit on the deficit. But phasing out the tax credit hits near-poor workers just like a tax hike—discouraging them from working longer hours or taking higher-paid jobs.

The best antipoverty strategy is to mix tax credits and minimum wages. At President Clinton's urging, Congress recently raised the tax credit. The next step is to raise the minimum wage by the modest amount the Senate Democrats have proposed. The Democrats should try again. Republicans supported such policies in the past. Perhaps Senator Dole can summon the will to do so this election year.

It's Simple: Hike the Minimum Wage, and You Put People Out of Work*

GARY S. BECKER

Higher labor costs reduce employment. That is why President Clinton's proposal to raise the federal minimum wage should be rejected. A higher minimum will further reduce the employment opportunities of workers with few skills.

Teenagers, high school dropouts, immigrants, and other low-skilled workers frequently earn less than $5.15 per hour, the proposed new minimum. They find employment in small establishments, especially in fast-food chains and other retail sectors. Increasing the minimum, as the President wants, would put some of them out of work since their productivity is not high enough to justify the cost to employers.

During the past several decades, many studies found that raising the minimum wage does reduce the employment of teenagers and others with low skills. But minimum-wage laws have remained popular among trade unionists and many politicians. And periodically, some economists have contested the prevailing wisdom about harmful effects.

*This article appeared in *Business Week*, March 6, 1995. Gary Becker is professor of economics at the University of Chicago.

SERIOUS FLAWS

A recent and widely cited challenge of this kind has come from several studies by two Princeton University economists, David Card and Alan B. Krueger—the latter now Robert B. Reich's chief economist at the Labor Department. One study finds that the change in employment after a minimum-wage hike is generally not bigger in states with a larger fraction of low-wage workers—the group that should be most affected by higher minimums.

Another study is frequently mentioned by Reich and others in the Administration to bolster the argument that a higher minimum does not lower employment. That study compares employment changes in fast-food restaurants in New Jersey and Pennsylvania after New Jersey raised its own minimum in 1992. Card and Krueger argue that because employment fell in Pennsylvania as much as it did in New Jersey, the drop in both states must have been due to other causes than the raise in the minimum.

There are some, and I am one of them, who believe that these studies have serious defects. Several of these were spelled out by Donald R. Deere and Finis R. Welch of Texas A&M University and Kevin M. Murphy of the University of Chicago in research they reported at the January meetings of the American Economic Association.

For example, the higher federal minimum in 1990 and 1991 caused a much larger drop in New Jersey's teenage employment than Pennsylvania's, which could explain why employment did not fall more in New Jersey when that state increased its own minimum in 1992. New Jersey employers presumably anticipated the increase in their state's minimum when they sharply cut employment in responding to the earlier wage hike.

DUELING STUDIES

The Card-Krueger studies are flawed and cannot justify going against the accumulated evidence from the many past and present studies that find sizable negative effects of higher minimums on employment. The Deere, Murphy, and Welch study shows that the two-stepped increase in the federal minimum from $3.35 to $4.25 in 1990 and 1991 reduced employment of teenagers, high school dropouts, and other groups with low earnings.

The magnitude of these reductions sounds about right, particularly after the authors take into account the economic recession of that time. After the 27% increase in the minimum wage, employment of male and female teenagers lowered by 12% and 18%, respectively, while employment of high school dropouts shrank by about 6%. If Congress raises the rate by 18%, to $5.15 an hour, these results imply that employment of workers with few skills will fall by over 5%.

President Clinton justified the need for a higher rate of pay by noting that a family cannot live decently on minimum-wage earnings. However, even Card and Krueger do not find that raising the minimum is an effective way to reduce poverty, since poor families typically get only a small fraction of their income from members whose wages are near the minimum.

The President also wants to increase current subsidization of the job training of less skilled workers, but these subsidies might be unnecessary if Clinton did not also advocate raising federal minimum wages. Higher minimums discourage on-the-job training of workers with few skills since they spend their time learning rather than producing.

Even a wizard would have a great deal of difficulty repealing the economic law that higher minimum wages reduce employment. Since politicians are not wizards, they should not try.

Dependency Is Our New Problem*

DANIEL PATRICK MOYNIHAN

In 1965, I published the first data that suggested that we might be moving into an era in which destitution in childhood, relatively independent of economic forces, would be our principal social problem. This was, I believe, a new proposition.

It dealt with dependency, the growing number of children born to single parents and dependent during childhood on what Pope John Paul II calls "the social assistance state." The U.S. Department of Labor came upon indications that the connection between child welfare and the workplace was breaking up. Earlier, when unemployment had dropped, new welfare cases dropped. No longer. Seemingly, dependency was an independent variable, possibly out of control.

This seemed especially so among minorities, a proposition I took to President Lyndon B. Johnson, who said as much in an address at Howard University in 1965. The president's analysis, however, was rejected. People said it wasn't so, and we could not prove otherwise. In truth, nothing much had yet happened. We had these indicators, but no more. And so we had to wait for the answer, or at least an approximate answer. We now have it. We were right.

*This article appeared in *Newsday*, October 18, 1991. Daniel Patrick Moynihan is New York's senior U.S. senator.

Specifically, we now know that of children born in the years 1967–69, some 22.1 percent were dependent on welfare (Aid to Families with Dependent Children, or AFDC) before reaching age 18. This breaks down to 15.7 percent for white children, 72.3 percent for black children.

What about the cohorts that followed? We don't finally know, but we can make an educated guess. The data tell us that children under the age of 8 were, on average, 36.8 percent more likely to have been on AFDC in the 1970s than their predecessors in the 1960s. If we assume that this same increase will show up for the whole of the 18 years (0–17), then we can project rates for children born as late as 1980. This gives us a white rate of 22.2 percent, and a black rate of 82.9 percent. (The latter would seem too high, and is, of course, only a projection. Still, we face the daunting possibility that five in six minority children are destitute and on welfare by age 18.)

This surely raises the issue of social justice—if, that is, it can be shown that such destitution in childhood is, in the main, a debilitating event. Not for each individual, but generally speaking for a class of individuals. Lawrence M. Mead of New York University believes this to be so. In "The New Dependency Politics" he writes: "The inequalities that stem from the workplace are now trivial in comparison to those stemming from family structure. What matters for success is not whether your father was rich or poor but whether you had a father at all."

This question has to be addressed: *Has* a new social condition appeared? Is something new going on? Are we missing something large? As an example, in February, 1991, some months before the report of the National Commission on Children appeared, the Senate Democratic Caucus had approved a legislative program entitled, "Strengthening America: The Democratic Agenda." A section on children included this passage: "There are some 64 million children in the United States. At current dependency rates, 16 million, or one-quarter, will be on welfare before they have reached the age of 18. . . . Children now make up the largest proportion of poor persons in the United States. There is no equivalent in our history to such a number or such a proportion.

"All this is new. This circumstance did not exist during the era of the New Deal, a half century ago. It did not exist during the era of the Great Society, a quarter century ago. It marks the emergence of a new issue in social policy. The issue of dependency."

However, before the document was sent to the printer, an "error" was spotted by the committee staff. The text that read: "This circumstance did not exist during the era of the New Deal, a half century ago. It did not exist during the era of the Great Society, a quarter century ago," was changed to read: "This circumstance was *not as recognized* during the era of the New

Deal, a half century ago, nor during the era of the Great Society, a quarter century ago" (emphasis added).

As I had written that passage, I asked about the change. It became transparently clear that those responsible had simply thought they were correcting a mistake. This is becoming the liberal orthodoxy: that there is nothing new. It is not, come to think, so very different from the views of those in the nineteenth Century who, on observing an industrial society all around them, could not conceive that society had changed to the extent that institutions needed to change as well. Thorstein Veblen called it "cultural lag."

My 1965 article [in the magazine *America*] began: "The United States is very possibly on the verge of adopting a national policy directed to the quality and stability of American family life." In this I was quite wrong. We did nothing of the sort. The evidence was rejected as inconclusive or worse. It is still rejected in the sense that orthodox opinion rejects the notion that there is anything qualitatively different about the present, insisting instead that the federal government simply do more of what we have been doing.

James S. Coleman of the University of Chicago traces our present situation back to the emergence of the corporation in medieval Europe and its gradual displacement of kinship structures. Is it possible that some general theory will come along that will tease out the sources of welfare dependency and get this problem back down to an acceptable level as Keynes did with unemployment? A reassuring thought, actually.

That would be for the long run. For purposes of the short run, it may be useful to note that in 1988 Congress enacted the Family Support Act, the first change in the welfare system since it was established as a federal program in the midst of that Great Depression. In recent Senate testimony, Judith Gueron, president of the Manpower Demonstration Research Corp., described the legislation: "The vision of welfare reform that we see reflected in the FSA [Family Support Act] is of a 'social contract' between poor parents and government, in which each party has responsibilities. Parents—both mothers and fathers—have the responsibility to contribute to the support of their children to the best of their abilities and to engage in activities designed to improve their self-sufficiency. The responsibilities of government are to provide the means for poor parents to become self-sufficient—such as employment services and supports—and to provide income when their best efforts fall short."

It remains to be seen whether the Family Support Act will be made to work. It is, in any event, only one of many measures that will be called for if, as is at the very least likely, the issue of dependency becomes the central issue of social justice in the next century. Come to think, millennium.

QUESTIONS FOR ANALYSIS

1. According to Professors Card and Krueger, their "findings call into question the standard model of the labor market that has dominated economists' thinking for the past half-century." Why?

2. Professor Becker maintains that the "Card-Krueger studies are flawed and cannot justify going against the accumulated evidence from the many past and present studies that find sizable negative effects of higher minimums on employment." Why does he believe that President Clinton's proposal to raise the minimum wage should be rejected? Do you agree? Why or why not?

3. Why does Professor Becker believe that the Card-Krueger studies are flawed?

4. The *New York Times* agrees with the Republicans that the minimum wage is a crude antipoverty tool. Why?

5. Do you think that the increase in the minimum wage should have occurred? Why or why not?

6. Senator Moynihan emphasizes that children now make up the largest proportion of poor persons in the United States. Why is he concerned about this fact?

7. Moynihan quotes with approval the following statement by Lawrence Mead: "The inequalities that stem from the workplace are now trivial in comparison to those stemming from family structure. What matters for success is not whether your father was rich or poor but whether you had a father at all." Do you agree? Why or why not?

8. What can the government do to influence family structure? What, if any, measures would you favor? Why?

PART FOUR

ANTITRUST

POLICY

For over a century, the United States has had antitrust laws on the books. In recent years, many have asserted that vigorous antitrust enforcement hurts innovation, which is so important to our economy. In the first article, Anne Bingaman, former head of the Antitrust Division of the U.S. Department of Justice, argues that this is not true. In the second article, the Antitrust Division describes eight recent cases.

Innovation and Antitrust*

ANNE K. BINGAMAN

It is a great pleasure to appear before the Commonwealth Club. You have long been recognized as the foremost public affairs speakers' forum in our nation, and I am enormously honored to be here. Today, I would like to address a topic particularly relevant in the Bay area—home to two of the greatest research universities in the world, the University of California at Berkeley and Stanford, and to hundreds, if not thousands, of high-tech companies. The world is envious and California makes this nation proud of the genius, drive, and products of those companies.

My subject is one often casually discussed and remarked upon, but, to my mind, not well enough understood—the relationship between the technological innovation so central to our economy, on the one hand, and vigorous, but sound, antitrust enforcement, on the other.

From time to time, it is asserted that vigorous antitrust enforcement hurts innovation by preventing the concentration of assets that spurs innovation. Competitive research is derided as duplicative and wasteful. Recently, the argument has been given an international flavor—it is asserted that the firms of other nations succeed because they are allowed to engage in cartel activity and collaborative research denied to U.S. firms because of the antitrust laws. As a general proposition, I believe that those views are wrong

*This is a speech given before the Commonwealth Club of California on July 29, 1994. Anne K. Bingaman was Assistant Attorney General.

and that innovation is *not* advanced by a policy of permitting cartel activity. Indeed, my core belief is that the U.S. economy today is the most dynamic, creates the most jobs, and produces the highest level of innovation precisely *because* we as a nation committed long ago to a policy of vigorous but sound antitrust enforcement. My thesis before you today, then, is that antitrust enforcement is as essential to innovation and economic growth in the twenty-first century as it has been in the twentieth—and that vigorous but reasonable antitrust enforcement is a crucial component of the fight to keep America competitive in international and high-tech markets.

Before I explain these views, however, it is imperative that you have a clear understanding of how modern antitrust law is applied. I need not go back to the legislative histories of the Sherman and Clayton Acts to ascertain whether those laws originally reflected an animus against large corporations. If they did, that is simply no longer the case. Congress drafted the antitrust laws in sufficiently general terms to delegate to the courts the task of developing an antitrust jurisprudence that is consistent with contemporary concepts of economic efficiency and consumer welfare. And the courts and federal antitrust enforcement agencies have accepted that responsibility.

As a result, current antitrust law recognizes the economic concepts of economies of scale and scope. Thus, on particular facts, a merger that eliminates competition between significant rivals may nevertheless pass antitrust muster if the parties truly can demonstrate that the merger is necessary to achieve substantial efficiency that will enhance consumer welfare. In the same vein, it is now clearly true that antitrust typically does not treat as inherently suspect horizontal or vertical joint ventures designed to integrate substantial business assets. This is especially true with respect to those types of joint ventures that are most directly involved in innovation. Despite the fact that such joint ventures had rarely been challenged under the antitrust laws, in 1984 Congress took action to lessen what was perceived to be an inhibitory effect of antitrust enforcement by making it clear that research and development joint ventures were to be judged under a rule of reason test. Last year, Congress took similar action with respect to production joint ventures. Whatever may have been the case previously, the time has long since passed when legitimate joint or collaborative activity among rivals could be viewed as inherently suspect under our antitrust laws.

With this understanding of contemporary antitrust policy firmly in mind, let me return to the original issue posed: is enforcement of modern antitrust policies that recognize economies of scale and scope, as well as the risk reduction benefits of collaborative action, inconsistent with the promotion of innovation? Lest you be left in doubt, for me the answer squarely is "no."

The economist Joseph Schumpeter was one of the first to articulate a theory that firms with stable and substantial market power were the most likely to invest in innovation. In particular, he suggested that firms with substantial market power—those that did not have to think in terms of short-range response to rivals—were the most likely to invest in long-range research and development. While not implausible as a matter of theory, Schumpeter's thesis has been severely undercut by real world developments, as Professor F. M. Scherer's 1984 book, *Innovation and Growth*, demonstrated. There, Professor Scherer showed that the largest corporations accomplish less in producing innovation than smaller enterprises, as measured by R & D expenditures, once some threshhold points are passed.

Further, in a world driven by rapid changes in technology, other empirical evidence available to us now indicates that the firms that prosper are more likely to be those that face fierce rivalry in their home markets than the sheltered monopolists. In a very real sense, it seems, the fear of being left behind is more likely to spur innovation than the security bred of stable market power.

This subject is extensively dealt with in Professor Michael Porter's recently acclaimed work, *The Competitive Advantage of Nations*. Noting that the need for antitrust enforcement has been questioned because of the globalization of industries and the view that domestic firms must merge or closely collaborate to gain economies of scale, Professor Porter found such claims to be inconsistent with available empirical evidence in the ten nations that he and his colleagues at the Harvard Business School studied. Rejecting arguments for lenient merger and cartel policies, he states that

in fact, creating a dominant domestic competitor rarely results in international competitive advantage. Firms that do not have to compete at home rarely succeed abroad. Economies of scale are best gained by selling globally, not through dominating the home market. . . . *Id.* at 662.

Observing that corporate managers often support lenient merger and collaboration policies because it is a "tempting way to raise short-term profits," Professor Porter views such policies as the path to national decline. Pointing to evidence that "active domestic rivalry is strongly associated with international success," he concludes that "a strong antitrust policy, especially in the area of horizontal mergers, alliances and collusive behavior, is essential to the role of upgrading any economy." *Id.* at 663.

Those of us who have spent our lives in antitrust were not surprised by Professor Porter's findings. The fundamental thesis of strong antitrust enforcement is that rivalry, not market power, fosters innovation and efficiency over the long run. For that reason, among others, this nation has committed its public policy for over a century to the view that antitrust enforcement promotes, rather than impedes, innovation. Innovation itself, of course, can and does take many forms. The term is applied to basic scientific breakthroughs, important commercial inventions, product modifications and new production techniques. All are important to society. Innovation, whether in the form of improved product quality and variety, or production efficiency that allows lower prices, is a powerful engine for enhanced consumer welfare. By prohibiting private restraints that impede entry or mute rivalry, antitrust seeks to create an economic environment in which the entrepreneurial initiative that is the hallmark of the U.S. economy can flourish, and opportunities for bringing innovations to market can continue to be exploited by the multitude of private actors in this freest of free market economies.

Acknowledging that an occasional natural monopoly may arise, and that enormous economies of scale may inevitably lead to few rivals in some markets, we remain skeptical about any general policy of eschewing rivalry in favor of collaborative research and development. This nation's experience teaches that innovation comes from unpredictable sources—from individuals and small firms as well as giant conglomerates. And this diversity in the sources of innovation is not limited to the nineteenth and early twentieth centuries, when change arguably occurred less rapidly.

If you compare the major firms in the computer and telecommunications industries in the 1950s, '60s, and '70s with the major firms today, you will see that rapid technological change can create opportunities for new entrants and individual achievement. It is not difficult to make a list of large U.S. firms who once possessed some degree of market power, only to fall back when confronted by more innovative rivals. It includes IBM, GM, big steel, major airlines, Citicorp, and you would undoubtedly think of additional examples. Happily, a number of those firms have demonstrated the ability to rebound, but their improved performance unquestionably was stimulated by the rivalry they have encountered.

The task of antitrust is not to prejudge winners but to make sure that private restraints do not narrow the potential sources of innovation. By preserving an economic climate that allows efficient sources of innovation to prosper, be they small or large, antitrust promotes the economic and sociopolitical values that have been the backbone of the success of the American economy.

An effective antitrust enforcement program promotes innovation by, among other things, reducing barriers to entry. When antitrust enforcement is a reality, potential entrants have less reason to fear market exclusion by existing firms. Antitrust enforcement can also act to prevent horizontal or vertical mergers that create non-efficiency based advantages for incumbent market leaders. For these and other reasons, potential entrants are more likely to invest the capital and effort needed for innovation when they have a "fair" chance at success, that is, when they have a chance to compete on the economic merits of their products or services.

We have brought two major cases in recent months to guarantee exactly this result. The first was against Pilkington, a British company that has maintained a monopoly throughout the world over the past three decades in float glass technology, the lowest cost method of manufacturing float glass used for automobiles and buildings.

While Pilkington may well have achieved its monopoly position fair and square—through patented innovations—it later cemented and abused its float glass technology monopoly through unfair and unlawful means. Among other things, Pilkington entered into patent and know-how license agreements with its principal rivals, which discouraged the very firms most likely to develop and use their own innovations in float glass technology. Pilkington continued to enforce against those would-be competitors very restrictive license provisions to thwart competition long after its patents had expired. As a result, Pilkington's major competitors—including such leading U.S. float glass manufacturers as PPG, Guardian and Ford—were largely foreclosed from the important international float glass technology market, and consumers were deprived of the benefits of more efficient production techniques and higher quality glass.

In May, the Department reached a settlement and proposed consent decree now before the U.S. District Court for the District of Arizona, that will end Pilkington's unlawful practices and thus free up the market in world float glass technology. We estimate that the settlement will not only stimulate innovation in this industry, but will generate anywhere from $150 million to $1.25 billion in exports through the year 2000 of American goods and services used to build new float glass plants coming on stream throughout the world. The *Pilkington* case is a paradigm for how U.S. antitrust enforcement can foster innovation and open export markets previously closed by anticompetitive practices.

On July 15, the Department filed a Complaint against, and a proposed settlement with, Microsoft for engaging in practices that we believed stifled innovation in another technology market: the market for operating systems used in personal computers.

Based on an extensive investigation, the Complaint alleges that Microsoft had gained a dominant position in its market by marketing operating systems that the public clearly wanted; but, as in *Pilkington,* Microsoft then chose to employ various unlawful practices to cement its dominance and thwart innovation.

In particular, the *Microsoft* Complaint challenges a combination of provi-

sions used by Microsoft in its license agreements with PC manufacturers—
"per processor" royalties that taxed competing operating systems, lengthy
terms, and huge minimum commitments, strictly enforced—that had the
effect of locking competing operating systems out of the market. While impeding competitors' access to the PC manufacturing channel, the Complaint further alleges that Microsoft also tried to get developers of
applications programs to sign non-disclosure agreements that would have
had the effect of preventing them from writing programs for those competing operating systems.

Our proposed consent decree, now before the United States District
Court in the District of Columbia, will end each and every one of these
challenged practices. It will also prevent Microsoft from engaging in other
practices, such as charging licensees on a lump sum basis or tying the sales
of its operating systems to other products—all practices that could produce
anticompetitive effects similar to the unlawful practices in which Microsoft
had previously engaged.

In short, the proposed *Microsoft* consent decree does precisely what the
antitrust laws are designed to do: provide a level playing field so that all
competitors have a fair shot at success on the merits.

Antitrust actions in previous Administrations have been central in promoting innovation and growth in the U.S. economy. The best, and most
important example in U.S. history is the challenge and eventual breakup of
AT&T—still an ongoing saga in Congress and before the United States District Court for the District of Columbia.

Prior to the Antitrust Division's challenge in that lawsuit, most of the nation was served by an integrated monopolist that faced little or no rivalry in
the various telecommunications markets in which it operated. The quality
of service provided by that integrated monopolist was not terrible; indeed,
it was considered to be good, at least when compared to that provided in
other countries by their monopoly providers. However, consumer choice
was hardly the hallmark of the integrated AT&T system. For the most part,
improvements appeared at a pace dictated by AT&T and its lengthy depreciation schedules, not by the needs of business or residential customers,
and certainly not by competition.

The divestiture required in the Modified Final Judgment in *U.S. v.
AT&T* separated the local telephone companies from AT&T's long-distance service and equipment manufacturing firms. The newly independent
local phone companies were required to provide access to AT&T's long distance rivals that was functionally equivalent to that provided to AT&T.
Other equipment manufacturers now had an opportunity to sell their
wares on the basis of quality, cost and efficiency to the divested local operating companies, AT&T's emerging long distance rivals, and users of telecommunications services.

In terms of innovation, the results have been spectacular. Fiber optic cable was promoted by Corning to Sprint and MCI. Advantages over the older cable technology for certain purposes are sufficiently clear that it is now widely deployed in local as well as long distance phone companies. The advances in fiber optics triggered responsive unexpected improvement in coaxial cable, through digital compression and other techniques. At the same time, satellite and other wireless technologies have advanced to offer still more options. How will these technologies be deployed in the Information Superhighway of the future? In what proportions will they be used? Which will be dominant? Which will be complementary? Which will be rendered obsolete? Nobody can speak with certainty on such issues. But one thing is clear—intelligent antitrust enforcement action served as a catalyst to technological innovation in telecommunications that is extraordinary by any measure. And the best technology is most likely to succeed in a competitive environment.

Antitrust has an important role in preserving the rivalry that spurs innovation. In addition to lowering barriers to entry, it can be used to prohibit collaborative conduct that is designed to, or has the effect of, retarding innovation. *U.S. v. Automobile Manufacturers Assoc. Inc.* (C.D. Cal. 1969), was a classic case of that type. The case, which was settled by consent decree, alleged that the major U.S. automobile producers entered into an agreement that required all members to grant royalty-free patent licenses to each other and to only take patent licenses from outsiders if all members could obtain the same license under the same terms. The effect of this agreement was to eliminate rivalry in pollution-abatement innovation. Since no one had to fear being left behind, the spur to innovate was blunted.

The Antitrust Division will continue to be alert to agreements designed to, or that have the effect of, retarding rivalry with respect to innovation, and will not hesitate to challenge them. At the same time, however, we offer a business review procedure that allows parties to obtain a statement of our enforcement intentions with respect to prospective conduct. Indeed, we recently issued a business review letter indicating that we would not challenge a joint venture designed to facilitate research on fuel cell development as an alternate energy source.

The arguments of those who endorse collaborative research and the development of national champions as the generally preferred method of advancement find little support in recent developments. Where commercial success depends on such ephemeral factors as consumer taste for services or products that do not yet exist and the pace and direction of new technology, there appears to be a definite advantage to fostering a competitive approach rather than developing a national champion. The history of HDTV technology development provides a vivid example. You may recall that both Japan and the European Community promoted a single chosen technological approach well in advance of technological readiness or clear expression of consumer desires.

By contrast, the U.S. approach was to promote rivalry in technological design. Initially, the chosen instrument approach to technology seemed to pay off, as both Japan and the EC developed prototypes before we did. However, there is often a difference between getting the quickest start and winning the race, a fact sadly recognized by Boston Red Sox fans over the years, and that is what appears to have happened with respect to HDTV development. At this point, neither the Japanese nor European systems have experienced any significant commercial success in their home markets. More importantly, there appears to be a growing consensus that a digital approach such as that developed by the various U.S. rivals will be superior to the analog systems utilized by the Japanese and Europeans.

I discuss the post-AT&T divestiture developments and the HDTV history as cautionary tales, not as proof that a chosen instrument approach to innovation can never succeed. I am not so presumptuous as to make such a categorical claim. These tales, however, and others that I will relate in a moment, reinforce my view that competitive markets are likely to be superior to government planning in bringing about innovation that will satisfy consumer tastes and needs.

The salutary effect of competition on innovation has been demonstrated repeatedly in this country when a variety of previously regulated industries have been deregulated, either in whole or in part. I have already talked about telecommunications in connection with the AT&T divestiture. But I would be remiss if I failed to credit at least part of the dynamism of that industry to the deregulatory actions of the FCC over the past twenty-five years. Deregulation of land and air transportation also has allowed consumers to reap the benefits of innovations in those fields. Freed of limitations on entry, trucking firms and airlines have deployed new and specialized types of equipment based on consumer desires and efficiency. In both of these fields, fierce service rivalry has produced substantial benefits to consumers. For example, the entry and subsequent growth of Southwest Airlines stimulated price competition that has benefited air travelers. Our securities industry provides another example of the benefits of competition. Since Congress reduced economic regulation of the securities industry, consumers of such services have saved hundreds of millions of dollars annually. Numerous strong firms compete for business on the basis of quality as well as price. Employing the latest developments in computer technology, they seek to provide consumers with added value.

In response to those who point to certain foreign successes as proof that a collaborative or chosen instrument approach to innovation is the better way, I make the following response. It is not foreign monopoly airlines that are seeking to exploit their superior efficiency by expanding international competition. Rather, it is our airlines, toughened by domestic rivalry, that are willing and anxious to compete on a global basis. Similarly, the U.S. telecommunications industry, both carriers and equipment manufacturers, is leading the way in attempts to modernize telecommunications capabilities around the world. And, while it is by no means a one-way street, U.S. banks and securities firms seem to be more willing and anxious to compete abroad than their foreign counterparts who have developed in a more sheltered environment. There are many other examples of industries in which the rough and tumble of U.S. competition has prepared our firms to play a leading role in international commerce. U.S. law firms, accounting firms, consulting firms, and advertising firms have all been, in general, more willing than their foreign counterparts to expand abroad. They have proved to be at least as adept as their foreign counterparts in innovating to meet the new and changing requirements of international trade.

Do not be misled by the fact that many of these examples involve services. Rivalry in domestic product markets also benefits U.S. manufacturers in their international efforts. Can there be any doubt that the relatively open U.S. automobile markets placed great pressure on U.S. auto firms to improve their products and efficiency? As a result, with better products, produced in factories that adopted recent innovations, the U.S. firms seem poised to regain international preeminence, or at least a place in the very first rank of auto producers. Telecommunications equipment, aircraft, agricultural equipment, pharmaceuticals, computers (hardware and software), medical equipment, and entertainment are other examples of U.S. products and services that excel in international competition at least in part because of the fierce quality rivalry that characterizes our domestic markets. Indeed, your own Silicon Valley is home to a company which has made the United States the world leader in the use of computers for animation, Silicon Graphics. Other U.S. companies, such as Lucas Films and Industrial Light and Magic, produce the computer-generated special effects that are seen in films such as Jurassic Park and Terminator 2. And many other industries and companies could be cited which have given this country a position in world markets second to none.

As you can plainly see, I have at least two strongly held beliefs: innovation is critically important to the advancement of this nation's economic interests; and, in general, the competitive approach is superior to the collaborative approach in terms of producing commercially valuable innovation. I do, however, want you to lose sight of some important qualifications to my general preference for competition in the effort to foster innovation. I have already noted them, but they bear repetition. I recognize that there may be situations in which collaboration in R&D or production may be necessary or simply more efficient than unilateral efforts. We are well aware of the benefits of risk reduction and economies of scale and scope that attend some joint ventures. In some rare instances, risk reduction or economies of scale may even justify a unified approach to research and development, but we will require those who promote that view to demonstrate why competition would be an inferior approach.

A similar reservation is appropriate with respect to government involvement in innovation. My celebration of the competitive benefits that usually flow to consumers from economic deregulation should not be viewed as denying *any* role to government. There is most definitely a role for government in the innovative process. The market does not do everything well. Appropriately, we do not rely solely on the market to protect us from unsafe products and workplaces, or from despoliation of the environment. In the same manner, government can provide an innovation vision, can suggest priorities, can provide an infrastructure through education and standardization, and in some cases can accelerate research in areas of potentially great value to society by providing planning and, in some instances, financial assistance. But, where consumer desires are uncertain, and the technology is as yet undeveloped, we should not lose sight of our experience—competition is generally the most effective means of promoting the innovation so critical to our nation's success in the international economic community of the twenty-first century. Sound, reasoned and vigorous antitrust enforcement can make its own significant contribution to that goal, and the Antitrust Division will remain a vital part of that effort.

Eight Recent
Antitrust Cases*

ANTITRUST DIVISION, U.S. DEPARTMENT OF JUSTICE

ONE: THERMAL FAX PAPER

After a two year investigation coordinated with Canadian antitrust officials, the Division and its Canadian counterpart in July 1994 brought criminal charges under their respective laws against an international cartel that had fixed prices in the $120 million a year thermal fax paper market. The Division's criminal information charged a Japanese corporation, two U.S. subsidiaries of Japanese firms and an executive of one of the firms with conspiring to charge higher prices to thermal fax paper customers in North America. Thermal fax paper is used primarily by small businesses and home fax machine owners. The defendants pleaded guilty and agreed to pay $6.4 million in fines.

The Division and Canadian officials are continuing the joint investigation into the fax paper industry under the U.S.-Canada Mutual Legal Assistance Treaty. This case was the Division's first criminal prosecution of a major Japanese corporation headquartered in Tokyo as well as the first to be coordinated with Canadian authorities, and illustrates the type of international antitrust cooperation that will occur more frequently in the future.

*This includes excerpts from the *Antitrust Division Annual Report for Fiscal Year 1994* (Washington, D.C.: Government Printing Office, 1995).

TWO: INDUSTRIAL DIAMONDS

In February 1994, the Division obtained an indictment of General Electric, DeBeers Centenary and two individuals charging them with conspiring to raise list prices in the $500 million a year industrial diamond industry. The two corporate defendants account for 80 percent of the industrial diamond market and allegedly fixed prices by secretly exchanging information about intended price hikes. The price increases went into effect worldwide in February and March of 1992. DeBeers and the two individuals remained overseas and beyond the reach of the U.S. courts. Trial of General Electric began in October 1994, but charges were dismissed after the presentation of the Government's case. The Division remains committed to aggressive criminal antitrust enforcement against international price-fixing cartels that raise prices to consumers and businesses in the United States.

THREE: GLASS MANUFACTURING TECHNOLOGY

In a major case designed to remove anticompetitive restraints imposed on American exports, the Division in May 1994 charged Pilkington, a British firm, and its U.S. subsidiary with monopolizing the flat glass market. The complaint alleged that Pilkington, which dominates the $15 billion a year international flat glass industry, foreclosed U.S. firms from foreign markets. Flat glass is used for windows and architectural panels by the construction industry and for windshields and windows by the automobile industry.

The Complaint alleged that Pilkington entered into unreasonably restrictive licensing arrangements with its most likely competitors, then over the course of almost three decades used these arrangements and threats of litigation to prevent American firms from competing to design, build and operate flat glass plants in other countries. By the time the Division filed its Complaint, Pilkington's patents had long since expired and its technology was in the public domain. A Consent Decree accepted by Pilkington to settle the case will bar it from restraining American and foreign firms who desire to sell their technology outside the United States. As a result, American firms will be able to compete for the 50 new glass plants expected to be built around the world over the next six years, resulting in an estimated increase in U.S. export revenues of as much as $1.25 billion during that period. This enforcement action builds on the Bush Administration's 1992 announcement that it would challenge such conduct and illustrates the Division's determination to address anticompetitive conduct that prevents

American firms from competing for business on fair terms in international markets.

FOUR: MILK AND DAIRY PRODUCTS CASES

As of September 30, 1994, the Division had filed 124 criminal cases against 73 corporations and 78 individuals in the milk and dairy products industry. To date, 63 corporations and 57 individuals have been convicted, and fines imposed total approximately $59 million. Twenty-seven individuals have been sentenced to serve a total of 4,774 days in jail, or an average of approximately 6 months. Civil damages assessed total approximately $8 million.

This sustained effort has broken up conspiracies that were illegally raising the price of milk supplied to children in public school districts across the country, including federally subsidized school lunch programs, as well as the price of dairy products supplied to the United States military. In FY 94, the division filed 18 criminal cases against 14 corporations and 11 individuals in the milk and dairy products industry. Seventeen grand juries in 14 states continue investigations in this industry.

FIVE: CELLULAR COMMUNICATIONS

In July 1994, the Division challenged the proposed acquisition by AT&T of McCaw Cellular, the nation's largest cellular telephone carrier, because this vertical merger could have raised prices and chilled innovation in cellular telephone services. These competitive concerns were addressed in a Consent Decree under which

□ long-distance rivals of AT&T will have access to McCaw systems equal to AT&T's access;

□ cellular rivals of McCaw that use AT&T equipment will continue to have access to necessary products and will be free of interference from AT&T should they wish to change equipment suppliers; and

□ AT&T and McCaw will not misuse confidential information obtained from AT&T equipment customers or McCaw equipment suppliers.

The Consent Decree allows the parties to seek the potential benefits of integration in cellular services but prevents abuse of their economic power in the cellular services, cellular long distance and telecommunications equipment markets.

SIX: PERSONAL COMPUTER OPERATING SYSTEMS

The Division in July 1994 charged Microsoft, the world's largest computer software company, with violating the antimonopoly provisions of Section 2 of the Sherman Act. Microsoft licensed its MS-DOS and Windows technology on a "per processor" basis that required personal computer manufacturers to pay a fee to Microsoft for each computer shipped, even if the computer did not contain Microsoft's software. Microsoft's dominant position in the market induced many personal computer manufacturers to accept these per processor contracts, which penalized the manufacturers if they dealt with Microsoft's competitors. The Division's Complaint further alleged that Microsoft's licensing contracts bound computer manufacturers to the contracts for an unreasonably long period of time. As a result of these practices, the ability of rival operating systems to compete was impaired, innovation was slowed and consumer choice was limited. Microsoft also imposed overly restrictive nondisclosure agreements on software companies that participated in trial testing of new software, thereby impeding the ability of those firms to work with Microsoft's operating system rivals.

Microsoft agreed to accept a Consent Decree that enjoins these and other restrictive practices, and the Decree was filed along with the Division's Complaint. The tentative settlement was reached in close cooperation with the competition enforcement authorities of the European Commission, which had been investigating Microsoft's conduct since mid-1993, and marked the first coordinated effort of the two enforcement bodies in initiating and settling an antitrust case.

SEVEN: DEPARTMENT OF DEFENSE PROCUREMENT

The division challenged as an unreasonable restraint on competition a "teaming arrangement" between Alliant Techsystems and Aerojet-General to supply the Department of Defense with cluster bombs. The two defendants are the only two U.S. suppliers of cluster bombs, and their agreement not to compete on the DOD contract raised the price of the bombs substantially. The Division negotiated a resolution that recoups $12 million for taxpayers on DOD's 1992 procurement—about a ten percent savings. The case stemmed from coordinated efforts by the Departments of Defense and Justice. The Departments have worked to formalize their cooperation on competition policy in the defense industry based on the recommendations of the Defense Services Board Task Force on Defense Mergers, an interagency working group in which the Division participated . . .

EIGHT: COLLEGES

During the prior Administration, the Division charged that the Ivy League universities and MIT had conspired to fix the prices that financial aid applicants paid to attend those schools. The government alleged that the defendants met regularly to avoid competing against each other in the amount of financial aid—that is, tuition discounts—offered to applicants. The Ivy League schools entered into a Consent Decree that prohibited such agreements. MIT chose to litigate the matter. After a trial in 1992, the district court ruled that MIT had violated the antitrust laws. The Court of Appeals for the Third Circuit subsequently remanded the case for further analysis.

In December 1993, the Division and MIT settled the case when MIT agreed to abide by certain standards of conduct in the future. Those standards allow MIT to agree on general principles for determining financial aid with other colleges that adhere to a need-blind admissions policy and that award students financial aid to meet their full needs. Under the standards, colleges may not agree on the amount or composition of aid offered to individual applicants, on tuition rates or on faculty salaries. In October 1994, Congress enacted legislation that allows colleges following need-blind admissions policies only a more limited form of cooperation on financial aid matters than were set forth in the MIT standards of conduct.

QUESTIONS FOR ANALYSIS

1. According to Assistant Attorney General Bingaman, the "fundamental thesis of strong antitrust enforcement is that rivalry, not market power, fosters innovation and efficiency over the long run." What evidence does she provide in support of this thesis?

2. Ms. Bingaman argues that an "effective antitrust enforcement program promotes innovation by . . . reducing barriers to entry." Why? Does the Pilkington case illustrate this point? If so, how?

3. She also says that the "arguments of those who endorse collaborative research and the development of national champions as the generally preferred method of advancement find little support in recent developments." What recent developments does she have in mind?

4. A central point of Ms. Bingaman's speech is that "innovation is critically important to the advancement of this nation's economic interests." Do you agree? Why or why not?

5. Does she argue that the government has no role in the innovative process? If not, what role does she regard as appropriate?

6. According to the Antitrust Division, an international cartel fixed prices in the thermal fax paper market. Why is this against the law?

7. The Antitrust Division challenged as an unreasonable restraint on competition a "teaming arrangement" between Alliant Techsystems and Aerojet-General to supply the Department of Defense with cluster bombs. Why?

PART FIVE

THE

ENVIRONMENT

Many people, including distinguished scientists and leading statesmen and stateswomen, are worried about what is happening to the environment; others feel that economic growth is being curtailed unnecessarily by alarmists who exaggerate the environmental risks. The first article, by Lester R. Brown of Worldwatch Institute, argues that our generation will be judged by whether we can reverse the environmental degradation of the planet. The second article, by President Clinton's Council of Economic Advisers, describes some of the environmental policies of the Clinton administration.

A New Era Unfolds*

LESTER R. BROWN

In early 1992, the U.S. National Academy of Sciences and the Royal Society of London issued a joint report that began: "If current predictions of population growth prove accurate and patterns of human activity on the planet remain unchanged, science and technology may not be able to prevent either irreversible degradation of the environment or continued poverty for much of the world."

It was a remarkable statement—an admission that science and technology can no longer ensure a better future unless population growth slows quickly and the economy is restructured. This abandonment of the technological optimism by two of the world's leading scientific bodies represents a major, though perhaps not surprising, shift—given the deteriorating state of the planet. A deepening concern about the future among scientists is indicated by their first-ever joint statement.

Despite the intensifying global interest in the planet's future, the U.N. conference on Environment and Development, convened last June in Rio de Janeiro, fell short of both hopes and expectations. Many of the difficulties centered on the U.S. insistence that goals and timetables for restricting carbon emissions be removed from the climate treaty, leaving it little more than a statement of good intentions. The convention designed to protect

*This article appeared in *Challenge*, May–June 1993. Lester R. Brown is president of Worldwatch Institute.

biological diversity had some flaws, but perhaps the most serious one was the missing U.S. signature. Yet, it was not a total loss by any means. The climate treaty, which was signed by 154 participating countries (including the United States), recognizes that global warming is a serious issue. And it does provide for setting up an international system for governments to report each year on changes in carbon emissions. This information flow itself will focus attention on the threat of climate change.

FLAWED ACCOUNTING SYSTEMS

The Rio conference presented an opportunity for taking stock of environmental gains and losses. Individual countries presented national state-of-the-environment reports, typically emphasizing their achievements. The descriptions included countless examples of local gains in achieving cleaner air and water, greater recycling of materials, and reforestation. These improvements notwithstanding, the broad indicators showed a continuing wholesale deterioration in the earth's physical condition. Since 1972, farmers have lost nearly 500 billion tons of topsoil through erosion—at a time when they were called on to feed 1.6 billion additional people. Atmospheric concentrations of carbon dioxide (CO_2), the principal greenhouse gas, climbed 9 percent. The risks to life on earth posed by the loss of stratospheric ozone and the associated increase of ultraviolet radiation—a threat not even imagined in 1972—were on everyone's mind.

These environmental concerns exist, in part, because of a misleading economic accounting system and a largely nonexistent biological accounting system. The internationally accepted system of national economic accounting used to calculate gross national product (GNP) rightly subtracts the depreciation of plant and equipment from the overall output of goods and services; but it takes no account of the depreciation of natural capital—such as the loss of topsoil from erosion, the destruction of forests by acid rain, or the depletion of the protective stratospheric ozone layer. As a result, the economic accounting system now used by governments greatly overstates progress. Failing to reflect reality, it generates environmentally destructive economic policies and is fragmentary at best.

No one knows how many species of plants and animals are lost each year, indeed, lacking a global inventory of the earth's biological resources, no one even knows how many species there are. Visual evidence from occasional national surveys and satellite data tell us that forests are disappearing in many countries. Similarly, incomplete data indicate that grasslands are deteriorating. Closely associated with the reduced grass and tree cover is the loss of topsoil. Despite the essential economic role of soil, no global data-gathering system measures its gains or losses. Nor does the biological accounting system warn when carrying-capacity thresholds are crossed. We learn that cattle numbers are excessive only when the rangeland begins to deteriorate. We discover that demands on forests are excessive only when they begin to disappear. We find that we have been overfishing only when the catch drops precipitously. Lacking information on sustainable yields, governments have permitted demands on these natural systems to become excessive, leading to their gradual destruction.

The result of this flawed economic accounting system and largely nonexistent biological accounting system is widespread degradation and destruction of the economy's environmental support-systems. Industrial firms are allowed to internalize profits while externalizing costs, passing on to society such expenses as those for health care associated with polluted air or those arising from global warming.

We can expect an expanding economy based on such an incomplete accounting system to slowly undermine itself, eventually collapsing as support-systems are destroyed. And that is *just* what is happening. The environmentally destructive activities of recent decades are now showing up in:

☐ reduced productivity of croplands, forests, grasslands, and fisheries;

☐ the mounting cleanup costs of toxic waste sites;

☐ rising health-care costs for cancer, birth defects, allergies, emphysema, asthma, and other respiratory diseases;

☐ the spread of hunger.

Rapid population growth, environmental degradation, and deepening poverty are reinforcing each other in a downward spiral in many countries. In its *World Development Report 1992,* the World Bank reported that per capita GNP had fallen in 49 countries during the eighties. Almost all these nations, containing 846 million people, are low-income, largely agrarian economies experiencing rapid population growth and extensive degradation of their forests, grasslands, and croplands. As the Royal Society/National Academy statement implies, it may not be possible to reverse this fall in living standards of nearly one-sixth of humanity if rapid population growth continues and existing patterns of economic activity are not changed. Just how difficult it will be is only now becoming clear. There is also a real risk that the demographic pressures and environmental deterioration that are replacing progress with decline will spread, enveloping even more of humanity during the nineties.

THE ECONOMIC COSTS

Many people have long understood, at least intuitively, that continuing environmental degradation would eventually exact a heavy economic toll. Unfortunately, no global economic models incorporate the depletion and destruction of the earth's natural support-systems. Only now can we begin to piece together information from several recent independent studies to get a sense of the worldwide economic effects of environmental degradation. Among the most revealing of these are studies on the effects of:

☐ air pollution and acid rain on forests in Europe;

☐ land degradation on livestock and crop production in the world's dryland regions;

☐ global warming on the U.S. economy;

☐ pollution on health in Russia.

These reports and other data show that the fivefold growth in the world economy since 1950 and the increase in population from 2.6 billion to 5.5 billion have begun to outstrip the carrying capacity of biological support-systems and the ability of natural systems to absorb waste without being damaged. In country after country, demands for crops and for the products of grasslands, forests, and fisheries are exceeding the sustainable yield of these systems. Once this happens, the resource itself begins to shrink as natural capital is consumed. Overstocking grasslands, overcutting forests, overplowing, and overfishing are now commonplace. Every country is practicing the environmental equivalent of deficit financing in one form or another. . . .

THE END OF RAPID GNP GROWTH

As noted earlier, our existing economic accounting system makes it difficult to assess the effect on the economy of both environmental degradation and the inherent constraints imposed by the carrying capacity of natural systems. We know that they will constrain future expansion of food and other essential commodities, but we do not know how much. Until we have an accounting system that incorporates natural-capital depreciation and losses, we cannot measure progress or decline accurately. For the time being, then, policymakers are forced to rely on GNP, which overstates progress.

More and more evidence indicates that the productivity of the earth's biological systems is emerging as a constraint on the growth of the economy and ultimately on that of population. This is most evident in the Third World, where the falling productivity of forests, grasslands, and, in some countries, croplands is reducing living standards.

In scores of developing countries, per capita grain production has been falling far longer than it has for the world as a whole. In Africa, the decline has been under way since 1970, dropping an average of roughly 1 percent a year. Such a decrease in a largely agrarian society is often followed by a decline in per capita GNP. Indeed, of the 49 countries where per capita GNP fell during the eighties, the great majority had experienced a drop in per capita-grain production. Globally, if growth in grain output cannot be raised from the 1 percent annually of the last several years to something close to the 3 percent a year that was helping eradicate hunger from mid-century until 1984, slow agricultural growth will become a severe constraint on world economic growth.

The production of beef and mutton on grasslands is also pushing against nature's boundaries. With rare exceptions, the world's grasslands are now either fully used or overused; in many areas they cannot sustain even the present output. A study of rangeland productivity in Pakistan's semiarid regions reports that overgrazing has reduced productivity to 15 to 40 percent of its potential. It describes the livestock sector as "caught in a downward spiral of too many sick animals chasing too little feed." Yet, putting more cattle and sheep in feedlots and expanding fish farming require more grain and soybean meal, further intensifying the competition with humans for grain.

As to forests, the demand for firewood and lumber exceeds forest regeneration by a wide margin in China, the Indian subcontinent, and semiarid Africa—areas that contain nearly half of humanity. Many developing countries that once exported forest products—such as Nigeri—are now importers. Of the 33 remaining Third World exporters of forest products, only 10 are projected to remain in that position by the end of this decade. With productive forests shrinking, the prospect for rapid long-term expansion of this sector is not good.

Agriculture also supplies industrial raw materials. Farms and forests together supply cotton and wool for the textile industries, leather for the leather goods industries, lumber for construction, wood pulp for paper, and many other basic inputs. Indeed, with the important exceptions of minerals and petrochemical products, virtually all the raw materials used in industry are of biological origin, coming from the agricultural and forestry sectors. Slower growth in world farm output thus affects not only the food prospect but the industrial growth prospect as well.

In addition to the constraints imposed by the maximum sustainable yield of forests, grasslands, and fisheries, the amount of fresh water produced by the hydrological cycle is impairing economic expansion in many countries. In more and more locations, the threefold growth in world water use since mid-century is pushing demand beyond the amount the hydrological cycle can supply. Water scarcity and falling water tables are now commonplace in the former Soviet Asian republics, the Middle East, North China, parts of India, North Africa, parts of sub-Saharan Africa, and the southwestern United States.

Pollution-cleanup costs are siphoning public capital away from investment in education, health care, and other key needs. Societies everywhere are facing huge cleanup costs for toxic chemical waste sites and areas contaminated with nuclear radiation. In some countries the costs have risen to billions of dollars; in larger industrial economies, such as the United States, they've surged to hundreds of billions.

The costs of environmentally induced illnesses, both those of health care and lost labor productivity, are mounting everywhere. We are only beginning to feel the effects. These illnesses cause an enormous drain on the financial resources of societies, and will take a heavy toll on labor-force productivity.

DECLINING GLOBAL GROWTH

Even a cursory glance at global economic growth, decade by decade, since mid-century shows the emergence of a disturbing trend for the world's poor (see Table 1). World economic growth exceeded that of population

TABLE 1   World Economic Growth by Decade, 1950–92

DECADE	ANNUAL GROWTH OF WORLD ECONOMY	ANNUAL GROWTH PER PERSON
1950–60	4.9%	3.1%
1960–70	5.2%	3.2%
1970–80	3.4%	1.6%
1980–90	2.9%	1.1%
1990–92	0.6%	−1.1%

Sources: World Bank, Department of Socio-Economic Data, unpublished printout, February 1992; International Monetary Fund, *World Economic Outlook*, October 1992; World Product in 1950 from Herbert R. Block; *The Planetary Product in 1980: A Creative Pause?*, U.S. Department of State, 1981; Population data from PRB, *World Population Data Sheets.*

by more than 3 percent during the fifties and sixties, providing a substantial gain in living standards for much of humanity. This was roughly cut in half during the seventies; it dropped even further during the eighties. And the nineties are not off to a good start. As a result of the global recession, per capita income fell by over 2 percent from 1990 to 1992. Even with a strong rebound, it could be mid-decade before incomes regain their 1990 level, giving the world five years with no improvement in living standards.

Now directly affecting national and global economic trends, environmental degradation can no longer be considered a peripheral issue. If destruction of the economy's support-systems continues, growth in economic output could fall below that of population, pulling average incomes down for the entire world. The world is entering a new era, one in which future economic progress depends on reversing environmental degradation. This, in turn, is contingent on new economic and population policies.

A NEW WORLD

It is evident that the existing economic system is slowly beginning to self-destruct as it undermines its environmental support-systems. The challenge is to design and build an economic system that is environmentally sustainable. Can we envision what this would look like? Can we devise a strategy for getting from here to there in the time that is available? The answer is "yes" to both questions.

The basic components of an effort to build an environmentally sustainable global economy are rather straightforward. They include:

☐ re-establishing climate stability;

☐ protecting the stratospheric ozone layer;

☐ restoring the earth's tree cover;

☐ stabilizing soils;

☐ safeguarding the earth's remaining biological diversity;

☐ restoring the traditional balance between births and deaths.

The future is replete with opportunities to reverse our current course:

☐ Traditional incandescent light bulbs, for example, would be replaced by the latest compact fluorescents, providing the same light but using only one-quarter as much electricity.

□ Solar energy is the only viable option to fossil fuels. It takes many forms: hydropower (already supplying one-fifth of the world's electricity), wind power, solar thermal power plants, firewood, photovoltaic cells, agricultural wastes, rooftop solar water heaters, alcohol fuels from sugar cane, and many more. All are likely to play a role.

□ The costs of photovoltaic cells are coming down fast; they are likely to play an important role eventually. The latest of these converts a phenomenal 22 percent of sunlight into electricity and produces it for 8¢ per kilowatt hour, well below the 12¢ for electricity from new nuclear plants in the state, but still above the 6¢ for that from coal-fired plants.

□ As costs continue to drop, the resulting cheap solar electricity permits the production of hydrogen fuel from the simple electrolysis of water. Hydrogen provides a means of both storing solar energy and transporting it efficiently over long distances, either by pipeline or by tanker, in much the same way that natural gas is transported.

□ Natural gas can serve as a bridging fuel, linking the fossil fuel era with the solar age. Shifting from coal or oil to natural gas sharply reduces air pollution and carbon emissions per unit of energy produced. And the facilities and pipelines now used to store and transport natural gas can one day be used for hydrogen.

□ There is a new awareness of the threat of unbridled population growth. Relating future population growth to the availability of cropland, fresh water, forest products, and grazing area along with the need for classrooms, health care, and jobs can serve as a guide to responsible policies.

One of the great tragedies of the last decade has been the withdrawal of all U.S. financial support for the U.N. Population Fund and the International Planned Parenthood Federation—the two principal agencies engaged in family planning internationally. This is one reason that up to 300 million of the world's women do not yet have access to family-planning services. Demographic surveys indicate that one in four births in the Third World is unplanned and unwanted. This fact explains, in part, the millions of street children there. Simply eliminating unwanted births would cut world population growth by more than one-third.

Glimpses of what our new world would look like can be seen here and there:

□ Japan has set the international standard for energy efficiency and, in the process, strengthened its competitive position in world markets.

☐ California, with its rapidly growing solar and wind industries, provides a window on future energy sources. Its solar thermal electric generating capacity of 350 megawatts and its wind generating capacity of 1,600 megawatts are enough to satisfy the residential needs of nearly 2 million people, easily enough for San Francisco, San Diego, and Sacramento combined.

☐ Thailand has halved its growth rate in less than 15 years.

☐ In the effort to stabilize soils, the United States' innovative Conservation Reserve Program (adopted in 1985) reduced soil erosion by one-third by 1990, and may cut it by another one-third by 1995.

☐ Germany has instituted a comprehensive program designed to force companies to assume responsibility for disposing of the packaging used with their products. Denmark has gone even further—banning unrefillable beverage containers.

In the end, we need not merely a vision, but a shared vision, one that guides and unites us in our day-to-day decision-making. Such a vision—a common blueprint—can infuse society with a sense of purpose as we try to build a new world, one much more attractive than today's. This sense of common purpose and excitement is essential if we are to create an environmentally sustainable economic system.

FACING UP TO CHANGE

The deterioration in living conditions for much of humanity during the eighties and early nineties will continue if economies are not restructured. It is in the largely agrarian economies that the link between deteriorating natural systems and living conditions is most direct, and the effects most visible.

At some point, the costs of deteriorating forests, dying lakes, damaged crops, respiratory illnesses, increasing temperatures, rising sea level, and other effects of fossil-fuel use become unacceptably high. Basic economics argues for a switch to solar energy. If the eventual consequence of failing to respond is catastrophe, the answer is obvious.

We are facing great change. There is little doubt of that. If we try to build the new economic system slowly, time will run out and environmental deterioration will lead to economic decline. The question is whether we will initiate the changes in time and manage the process, or whether the forces of deterioration and decline will prevail, acquiring a momentum of their own.

And since we have little experience in the modern era with which to judge it, we cannot be certain what the deterioration/decline scenario would look like.

The challenge is not only about what we need to do, but how we can do it quickly—before time runs out and the entire world is caught in the downward spiral that already has roughly one-sixth of humanity in its grip. Among the principal policy instruments that can convert a slowly self-destructing economic system into one that is environmentally sustainable are regulations and tax policy. Until now, governments have relied heavily on regulation, but the record of the last two decades shows that this is not a winning strategy.

Regulations clearly do have some role to play. They are needed in the handling of toxic waste and radioactive materials—things too dangerous to leave to the marketplace. Environmentally damaging chemicals, such as CFCs, can be banned. Energy efficiency standards for automobiles and household appliances can cut carbon emissions, air pollution, and acid rain.

By far the most effective instrument to transform the economy quickly, however, is tax policy, specifically the partial replacement of income taxes with environmental taxes. And tax policy permits the market to work unimpeded, preserving its inherent efficiency. Today, governments tax income because it is an easy way to collect revenue, even though it serves no particular social purpose. Replacing a portion of income taxes with environmental taxes would help to transform the economy quickly. This shift would encourage work and savings and would discourage environmentally destructive activities. In short, it would foster productive activities and discourage destructive ones, guiding both corporate investments and consumer expenditures.

Among the activities that ought to be taxed are the burning of fossil fuels, the production of hazardous chemical waste, the generation of nuclear waste, pesticide use, and the use of virgin raw materials. The adoption of a carbon tax, which would discourage the burning of fossil fuels, is now being actively considered in both the European Community and Japan. Even a modest carbon tax would quickly tip the scales away from investment in fossil-fuel production and toward investment in energy efficiency and renewable energy sources. Within a year of adoption of an international carbon tax, literally scores of solar thermal plants could be under construction.

The measure of individuals or nations is whether they respond to the great issues of their time. For our generation, the great issues are environment and poverty. We will be judged by whether we can reverse the environmental degradation of the planet and eradicate the dehumanizing poverty that is now engulfing more and more of the world's people.

We know what we have to do. And we know how to do it. If we fail to convert our self-destructing economy into one that is environmentally sustainable, future generations will be overwhelmed by environmental degradation and social disintegration.

Simply stated, if our generation does not turn things around, our children may not have the option of doing so.

Addressing Environmental Externalities*

Joseph E. Stiglitz

PRESIDENT CLINTON'S COUNCIL OF ECONOMIC ADVISERS

The notion of tradeoffs is among the most fundamental in economics: nothing is free; everything has an opportunity cost. In private markets, tradeoffs are handled automatically, as consumers choose among alternative goods and services and producers choose among alternative inputs. Prices guide these decisions. Tradeoffs involving the environment cannot be made so easily, however, because use of the environment is generally unpriced. As a result, firms and individuals, in their marketplace decisions, do not always make the best tradeoffs from the standpoint of society as a whole. The effects of failing to price environmental goods and services are examples of externalities (Box 1). When externalities are significant, the government can often design policies that improve the functioning of markets and thereby increase aggregate social welfare.

The Administration has sought to encourage the development of environmental technologies to mitigate tradeoffs and foster economic growth. Improvements in the technologies for preventing and treating pollution, and efforts to spread knowledge about technologies already available, can free resources for other socially beneficial purposes or permit the attainment of higher environmental goals without increasing the burden on the economy. Given the worldwide explosion in environmental regulatory ac-

*This is an excerpt from the *Economic Report of the President* (Washington, DC: Government Printing Office, 1994).

BOX 1   **EXTERNALITIES**

An externality, or spillover, is a type of market failure that arises when the private costs or benefits of production differ from the social costs or benefits. For example, if a factory pollutes, and neither the firm nor its customers pay for the harm that pollution causes, the pollution is an externality. In the presence of this negative (harmful) externality, market forces will generate too much of the activity causing the externality, here the factory's production, and too much of the externality itself, here the pollution. In the case of beneficial externalities, firms will generate too little of the activity causing the externality, and too little of the externality itself, because they are not compensated for the benefits they offer. For example, the development of laser technology has had beneficial effects far beyond whatever gains its developers captured, improving products in industries as diverse as medicine and telecommunications. Too little research and development and other activities generating positive externalities will take place in the absence of some governmental intervention.

To remedy market failures and induce the market to provide the efficient level of the externality-causing activity, the private parties involved in the activity must face the full social costs and benefits of their actions. Policymakers may employ a variety of tools to accomplish this result, such as taxes, user fees, subsidies, or the establishment or clarification of property rights.

tivity—in the Far East, in eastern Europe, in Mexico, and elsewhere—the development of more effective and lower cost pollution control technology can also increase our export competitiveness. In fact, we already enjoy considerable success in this area. The United States is now the world leader in exports of environmental equipment. In a global market for environmental technologies of $295 billion in 1992, the $134 billion U.S. share is the largest by far. Our trade surplus in pollution control equipment has been increasing and was $1.1 billion in 1991.

The Administration has also sought to improve the "technology" of regulating the use of natural and environmental resources. This effort involves seeking a better balance among conflicting interests in the use of natural resources, and developing approaches to regulate pollution that rely more on economic incentives and eliminate the economic distortions of some current regulations. Examples of improving the technology for regulating the environment are found in the Administration's plan for managing the old growth forests of the Pacific Northwest, in its approach to grazing on Federal lands, in the Climate Change Action Plan, and in the Administration's position favoring the reauthorization of the Comprehensive Environmental Response, Compensation, and Liability Act, better known as

"Superfund." To better assess where interventions to improve the environment will benefit the economy, the Administration is also engaged in efforts to define sustainable development and develop "green" GDP accounts.

MANAGING RESOURCES ON FEDERAL LANDS

The Federal Government owns vast tracts of land, primarily in the West. These lands contain natural resources of economic importance to both local communities and the Nation, including timber and other forest products, forage for grazing livestock, and mineral deposits. They are also sources of extremely valuable environmental amenities, such as open space for recreational uses like wildlife viewing, scenery, camping, hiking, and hunting; fish and wildlife (including endangered species) habitat; watershed protection; and many others.

Improving the "technology" of regulating the use of these Federal lands is a centerpiece of Administration policy. Two principles guide that policy: (1) reducing inefficiencies caused by improper pricing and regulatory restrictions, and (2) ensuring that both pricing and regulation will achieve a better balance among competing uses of these resources, particularly between extractive (timber, grazing, mining) and environmental uses. These principles can be seen at work in the Administration's plans for managing old growth forests in the Pacific Northwest and for rangeland reform.

Old Growth Forests, Spotted Owls, and Timber

The controversy over logging in the old growth forests and spotted owl habitat of the Northwest provides a case study in reconciling environmental and economic objectives and illustrates how a careful balancing of competing interests can result in progress on all fronts.

The forest products industry is a major industry in the Pacific Northwest, where it is heavily dependent on timber from Federal lands. Much of the Federal land on which this logging has taken place consists of mature forest stands. Referred to as "old growth," this mature forest is the habitat of the northern spotted owl, a threatened species, and many other plants and animals.

For several years Federal forest policy in the Northwest failed to take appropriate account of impacts on environmental quality and biodiversity. In particular, timber harvests on Federal lands were accelerated substantially in the mid- and late 1980s: Such harvests in the habitat of the spotted owl rose from 2.4 billion board feet (bbf) in 1982 to 6.7 bbf in 1988. According to experts, these levels were too high to be sustained indefinitely. Legal challenges to Federal timber policy resulted in injunctions blocking the sale of timber on Federal forest lands in the spotted owl region, in part because agencies within the Federal Government had failed to work cooperatively to comply with environmental and forest management laws. The injunctions had a severe impact on the timber industry, albeit in large part because harvest levels had been extraordinarily and unsustainably large.

The Administration put a high priority on resolving the problems associated with forest management policy in the Pacific Northwest. Accordingly, in July 1993, the Administration announced a "Forest Plan for a Sustainable Economy and a Sustainable Environment." The plan attempts to end the uncertainty caused by legal wrangling and confusion and ameliorate the impact of economic dislocation, while achieving full compliance with existing laws. It also seeks to maintain and improve the ecosystem as a whole, balance the interests of competing uses of the ecosystem for environmental and economic purposes, and create a political consensus to avoid economic instability.

The plan provides for the maximum legally defensible harvest from Federal forests in the spotted owl region (about 1.2 bbf annually). The process of adjustment to the new, lower harvest levels will be smoothed by an economic adjustment plan that is expected to create more than 8,000 new jobs and 5,400 retraining opportunities in the region in 1994. Many of the new jobs will be in enterprises that improve water quality, expand the prospects for commercial fishing, and improve forest management in the region.

The plan focuses on maintaining and improving the environmental quality of watersheds in the region, recognizing how the complex interactions of flora, fauna, and human activities affect that ecosystem. It establishes old growth reserves and protects over 6.5 million acres of old growth forest (about 80 percent of existing old growth). It also establishes 10 "adaptive management areas" for experimentation into better ways of integrating ecological and economic objectives.

Rangeland Reform

The Federal Government owns extensive rangelands throughout the West. While these lands are used primarily for grazing cattle and sheep, increased demand for environmental uses has fueled controversy over Federal management. The controversy over rangeland reform shows the importance of integrating pricing with regulation to use the Nation's resources more efficiently and strike a better balance between economic and environmental objectives.

A central point of contention involves the fees that the Federal Government charges ranchers to graze animals on Federal land. These fees should reflect both the value of the forage used by an additional animal and the external environmental costs of grazing an additional animal (such as the value of reductions in recreation or water quality). Charging ranchers the marginal value of forage, the first component, encourages efficient use of the range. By preventing overgrazing, it protects the condition of the range for future grazing uses. It also promotes long-run efficiency in the livestock industry: Prices for forage that are too low encourage excessive investment in the industry. Forage value varies from tract to tract because of differences in forage productivity, location, proximity to roads and other transportation, rainfall, and access to water. But it can still be measured easily and reliably using the value of private rangelands in nearby locations. The second component, the external costs of grazing, cannot be determined from private market transactions. But economists have developed ways of inferring the value of open space or other environmental amenities from the costs people willingly incur to use them or from sophisticated survey methods.

Current Federal management policies are relics of an earlier era when the Federal Government used resource subsidies to encourage settlement of the West. One result is that grazing fees on Federal lands average only 17 to 37 percent of the value of grazing on comparable private lands. Moreover, the formula used to calculate Federal grazing fees has kept those fees from increasing along with private grazing lease rates. Promoting efficiency thus means both increasing grazing fees and ensuring that Federal grazing fees change from year to year in accordance with changes in rent on private grazing land. The Administration's plans for rangeland reform do both. The current proposal calls for phasing in a new fee structure that more than doubles current fees, and for using an updating formula that will adjust Federal fees at the same rate that private fees change.

Pricing reform must be accompanied by changes in regulation. For example, Federal grazing permits have "use-it-or-lose-it" provisions, under which decreases in the number of animals grazed may result in the loss of a grazing permit or a reduction in the number of animals that the permitholder may graze in the future. This policy prevents ranchers from temporarily reducing the number of animals grazed to improve range condition. The Administration's plan allows the terms of grazing permits to be rewritten to allow ranchers to vary the number of animals they graze in response to changes in weather or economic conditions. The plan also includes provisions to strengthen environmental management.

CLIMATE CHANGE ACTION PLAN

Certain gases emitted into the atmosphere by industrial, automotive, and other combustion have been implicated as a threat to the global climate: By preventing reflected solar radiation from escaping into space, these "greenhouse gases" may be causing a generalized warming of the planet. For this reason, an international agreement to reduce greenhouse gas emissions, the Framework Convention on Climate Change, was signed in 1992. The previous Administration had adopted what was called a "no regrets" policy; it was willing to take steps to reduce emissions only if those actions would be beneficial for other reasons—that is, even if greenhouse gas emissions were ultimately found unrelated to changes in the global climate. In contrast, this Administration sees cost-effective policies to reduce greenhouse gas emissions as appropriate "insurance" against the threat of climate change. Accordingly, the President, in his Earth Day speech on April 21, 1993, issued a "clarion call" for the creation of a cost-effective plan to reduce U.S. greenhouse gas emissions to 1990 levels by the year 2000.

The President's call resulted 6 months later in the Climate Change Action Plan, containing nearly 50 initiatives that cover reductions in all significant greenhouse gases and will affect most sectors of the economy. The plan was based on the understanding that the climate change threat results from *all* greenhouse gases, that it depends on *net* emissions (after accounting for greenhouse gas "sinks" such as forests and oceans), and that the problem is *global*. The strategies adopted to address the externalities associated with greenhouse gas emissions were chosen on the basis of a qualitative assessment of the cost-effectiveness of the alternatives, in part by selecting policies that make markets work better.

Some of the strategies expand upon initiatives of this and previous Administrations to promote energy-saving technology. For example, the Green Lights program improves the diffusion of technology by providing consumers and firms with information about environmentally friendly products such as energy-saving lights that promise to reduce electricity generation and the resulting emissions. Other strategies reduce emissions by making government more efficient. Two examples are (1) reform of regulations that block the seasonal use of natural gas (a low-polluting alternative to coal) by electric utilities, and (2) removal of regulatory impediments to private investments in upgrading Federal hydroelectric facilities.

Parking Cashout

Greenhouse gas emissions will also be reduced by improving the pricing of activities that generate externalities. The parking cashout policy attempts to correct a distortion in private incentives resulting from the tax treatment of employer-provided parking. Currently, the Internal Revenue Code allows employers to deduct any costs for employer-provided parking as a business expense, and lets workers exclude the benefits from their taxable income (up to $155 a month). As a result, 95 percent of automobile commuters receive free or subsidized parking, more than half of them in central business districts. All told, U.S. companies claim $52 billion per year in parking-related deductions from this free or subsidized service.

The Climate Change Action Plan proposes that Federal tax laws be modified to require that firms offer employees the option of taking the cash value of their employer-provided parking benefit as taxable income rather than accepting their free parking space. The program would apply initially only to those firms with more than 25 employees that make monthly cash payments for their employees to park in lots owned by third parties. Thus, only about 15 percent of employer-provided parking would be covered at first, although the program would expand later as new parking leases are negotiated.

This policy change should reduce the overuse of automobiles for commuting resulting from the current parking subsidy, by making commuters face more of the social costs of driving. As consumers shift to carpools and public transportation, greenhouse gas emissions, other pollutants, and traffic congestion should all be reduced. Other distortions of the choice between commuting by car and by public transit will remain uncorrected, however, to the extent that current regulation of automobile emissions does not fully capture their environmental, congestion, and health costs.

International Strategies for Greenhouse Gas Reductions

One hundred and sixty-one countries signed the Framework Convention on Climate Change in 1992, agreeing that it is necessary to stabilize greenhouse gas concentrations at a level that will prevent "dangerous anthropogenic interference with the climate system." Because this is a global problem, the Climate Change Action Plan addressed what is termed "joint implementation"—the cooperative effort between countries or entities within them to reduce greenhouse gas emissions. The plan recognizes that there may be enormous cost savings to meeting global goals for greenhouse gas reductions if acceptable international strategies can be developed to reduce emissions where it is cheapest to do so, rather than have each country pursue its emissions reduction goals on its own. Some important questions need resolution, however, such as how reductions are to be identified, monitored, and enforced. To begin testing the joint implementation concept, the plan creates a pilot program that evaluates investments by U.S. firms and government assistance to foreign countries for new greenhouse gas emission reductions; measures, tracks, and scores these reductions; and, in general, lays a foundation for broader, more formal policy initiatives in the future.

SUPERFUND REAUTHORIZATION: THE ADMINISTRATION POSITION

The Comprehensive Environmental Response, Compensation, and Liability Act, better known as Superfund, was enacted in 1980 and amended in 1986 in response to widespread concerns that improperly disposed-of wastes threatened human health and valuable natural resources, such as groundwater aquifers. The act has been unsatisfactory in addressing this problem. Fewer than 20 percent of the 1,300 disposal sites on the priority list drawn up by the Environmental Protection Agency (EPA) have been fully "cleaned up," although 3,500 separate actions have been taken to remove wastes posing an immediate threat to health.

At the same time, the costs of the program have been substantial, running almost $7 billion per year. This figure includes direct draws on the Superfund trust fund collected from the oil and chemical industries to pay for EPA expenses (including $1.6 billion in spending on cleanups where no private parties can be assigned responsibility), $3.2 billion in spending by Federal agencies that own or contributed to hazardous waste sites, and $2 billion in spending by private parties, much of which goes to lawyers' fees and other transactions costs in an effort to escape or reduce liability. Some estimates put the total cost of cleaning up the 3,000 sites projected to be on the EPA's National Priority List (NPL) over the next 30 to 40 years at $130 billion to $150 billion, with $200 billion to $300 billion more needed for Federal facility cleanups.

In response to the poor cost-effectiveness and slow pace of this program, the Administration has proposed several significant reforms. The two most important involve the standards and processes governing the cleanup strategy chosen at a site, and the process for assigning and financing liability.

Remedy Selection

Under the current law, remedial measures at Superfund sites are chosen with a preference for treatment and permanent cleanup of soil and water. They are also selected to meet high standards of cleanliness: land generally must become suitable for residential use, and water often must achieve drinking quality. Costs have little weight in remedy selection; they come into play only to identify the cheapest of the set of remedies meeting other criteria.

The Administration's position establishes more reasonable goals and processes for cleanup decisions. It sets uniform national goals for health and environmental protection to guide remedy selection. It substitutes a concern for long-term reliability as a factor to consider in remedy selection, in place of the preference for treatment and permanence (except for treatment of "hot spots"). It explicitly recognizes containment as a legitimate cleanup strategy. It limits the use of State and Federal standards designed for other pollution contexts. Finally, it introduces greater flexibility and community input into the determination of appropriate land use for the site, permitting some sites to be designated for industrial use, with appropriately lower levels of cleanup required.

The Administration's proposal also offers a streamlined approach to remedy selection at individual sites. With EPA approval, parties will be able to avail themselves of a set of cost-effective "generic" remedies established by the EPA that apply to certain frequently encountered types of waste disposal problems. Alternatively, they can formulate designs that meet national cleanup levels that are based on realistic assumptions and practices concerning risks. If the party liable for cleanup believes it can devise an even cheaper remedy that can meet the national health standards, it can perform a site-specific risk analysis to make its case to EPA. This option allows parties to propose remedies based on the ultimate goal of protecting health and the environment, rather than on the "intermediate" targets of reductions in soil or water concentrations, and helps tailor remedies chosen for a site to its particular features.

Most important, a factor in the remedy selection process at individual sites will be a comparison of the reasonableness of costs against several measures of effectiveness. This approach introduces discipline, transparency, and recognition of tradeoffs into the remedy selection process, while retaining consideration of other factors such as community acceptance and meeting the primary criterion of protecting health and the environment. Cost will also be considered in decisions on whether to defer final cleanups for cases where a new technology is on the horizon to replace a current one that has disproportionately high costs.

The Liability System

The transactions' costs associated with cleanups, especially litigation expenses, have been massive under current law. One study found that these costs account for 19 to 27 percent of all Superfund costs. Transaction costs are substantial in part because liability under current law is strict, joint and several, and retroactive: A party that contributed waste to a site used by others can be held liable for the entire cost of cleanup, and a party is liable for the results of its dumping even if its action was legal at the time. As a result, potentially responsible parties (PRPs) have strong incentives to contest their liability (resulting in high enforcement costs to the EPA), to sue other PRPs to recover costs, and to sue their insurance companies when the latter refuse to pay related claims.

The Administration's proposal seeks to limit these transactions' costs by streamlining the liability allocation process and making it more fair. The new allocation process is based upon nonbinding arbitration, in which PRPs are assigned a share of liability based on factors such as the volume and toxicity of their wastes. PRPs who settle for their assigned shares would surrender their rights to pursue other PRPs for contribution, be protected from suits by other PRPs, and be offered, for a fee, protection from future liability arising from remedy failure or undiscovered harms. As an added incentive to settle, the EPA would pay settling parties for their share of the "orphan shares"—the share of liability attributed to an identified but insolvent party—but nonsettling parties could still be held liable for all or part of the "orphan share."

The Administration proposal also addresses the growing problem of Superfund-related insurance litigation. The problem arises because insurance contracts written before Superfund was enacted did not expressly allocate Superfund liabilities. Subsequently, courts in some States have interpreted those contracts to require insurance companies to assume most Superfund liabilities, but courts in some other States have held the opposite. The scope of insurers' liability in most States is undecided. Building on a proposal originally suggested by the insurance industry, the Administration proposal calls for creation of an Environmental Insurance Resolution Fund financed through fees and assessments on property and casualty insurers. If the PRPs can show sufficient insurance coverage before 1986, the fund would be used to settle their insurance claims for cleanup and restoration costs at pre-1986 NPL sites, as well as some costs at non-NPL sites, at rates determined simultaneously for all of a PRP's sites. The combination of the allocation process and the insurance settlement process should substantially reduce transactions costs and increase fairness.

QUESTIONS FOR ANALYSIS

1. What is the role of externalities in causing environmental pollution?

2. What techniques can the government use to reduce pollution? What are the relative advantages and disadvantages of each of these techniques?

3. According to Mr. Brown, "The internationally accepted system of national economic accounting used to calculate gross national product [or gross domestic product] . . . rightly subtracts the depreciation of plant and equipment from the overall output of goods and services, but it takes no account of the depreciation of natural capital—such as the loss of topsoil from erosion, the destruction of forests by acid rain, or the depletion of the protective ozone layer." Is this true? Explain.

4. In Mr. Brown's view, "Basic economics argues for a switch to solar energy. If the eventual consequence of failing to respond is catastrophe, the answer is obvious." What would be the costs to society of such a transition? What would be the benefits? Would the costs and benefits depend on how quickly the switch was made? Are you in favor of such a switch? Why or why not?

5. Mr. Brown argues that: "By far the most effective instrument to transform the economy quickly . . . is tax policy, specifically, the partial replacement of income taxes with environmental taxes." What sort of environmental taxes does he have in mind? What groups would be hurt most by such taxes? Would you favor the partial replacement of income taxes with environmental taxes? Why or why not?

6. According to President Clinton's Council of Economic Advisers, the fees that the federal government charges ranchers to graze animals on federal land "should reflect both the value of the forage used by an additional animal and the external environmental costs of grazing an additional animal (such as the value of reduction in recreation or water quality)." Why? Aren't federal lands a resource that should be used? Don't ranchers help to pay for federal lands through their tax payments?

7. President Clinton's Council of Economic Advisers criticizes existing government regulations whereby "Federal grazing permits have 'use-it-or-lose-it' provisions, under which decreases in the number of animals grazed may result in the loss of a grazing permit or a reduction in the number of animals that the permitholder may graze in the future." What is wrong with such permits? If the holder of a permit makes little or no use of it, why should he or she continue to have this privilege? Isn't the basic idea to make maximum use of federal lands?

8. President Clinton's Council of Economic Advisers supports a requirement "that firms offer employees the option of taking the cash value of their employer-provided parking benefit as taxable income rather than accepting their free parking space." What is this proposed requirement meant to achieve? Do you think it will work? Why or why not?

9. Is it likely that international cooperation will be required to reduce the emission of greenhouse gases? Why or why not? What problems are likely to be encountered in obtaining such cooperation?

10. From the point of view of society as a whole, shouldn't environmental pollution be eliminated completely? After all, our planet can only tolerate so much in the way of pollutants, and it is common knowledge that air pollution in cities like Los Angeles and water pollution in areas like the Chesapeake Bay are very high. Isn't it obvious that we should put a halt to environmental pollution?

PART SIX

FARM POLICY

Agriculture is an important industry in the United States, and it has been heavily influenced by a variety of government regulations. The first article is a newspaper account of the record grain prices in early 1996, the highest in decades. The second article, from another newspaper, describes some of the changes in 1996 in federal legislation affecting the country's farms. The third newspaper article attacks the practices of the Pennsylvania Milk Marketing Board, an independent agency operating with state authority.

New Growth on the Old Farm*

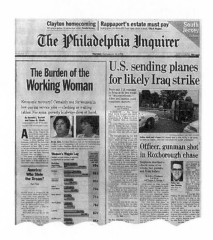

PHILADELPHIA INQUIRER

There's frenzy in the grain markets. Wheat prices are soaring. Corn prices are shattering records. And Agriculture Secretary Dan Glickman is watching it unfold with a nervous smile.

"It's the kind of market that I've always said I wanted," Glickman said in a recent interview. "I've argued for higher [grain] prices, and, certainly, grain farmers said we've priced our product too low. So, from that standpoint, it's positive."

Not in 20 years has agriculture seen anything like this: record crop prices, booming farm exports, raucous grain markets, and farmers planting fence-row to fence-row.

It's a volatility that epitomizes the new world of American farming. For years, the U.S. Department of Agriculture, because of chronic overproduction, required farmers to idle farmland. Those rules ended with a new farm law, signed earlier this month.

Large government storehouses of grain? They're gone, too. Grain export subsidies? They've been discontinued. And iron-clad conservation programs that idled more land? Glickman altered those to allow planting on some better-quality cropland.

But he knows the current boom can have bad side effects. Grain farmers obviously welcome high prices. But such grain users as livestock producers

*This article, by Tom Webb, appeared in the *Philadelphia Inquirer,* April 13, 1996.

and food processors are being trapped in a nasty price squeeze—and are worried that grain bins are so empty, it may become hard to buy grain at any price.

And there's growing concern about drought. "If you don't have a crop, high prices aren't as helpful," Glickman said. "And, certainly, if you're in the livestock business, it can put you under some degree of stress. But by and large, these are better problems to have than perennially low prices."

In the year since Glickman took office, corn prices are up about 90 percent and wheat prices up about 75 percent—all with almost no effect on consumer food prices.

CHART 1 Wheat

Futures contract on the Chicago Board of Trade, for delivery in May 1996.

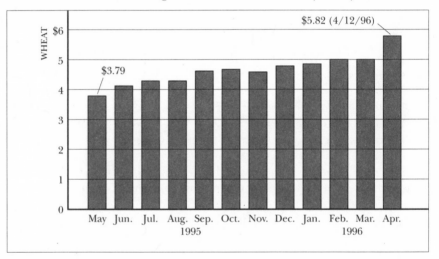

Corn prices have shattered records several times in recent trading days and now are at more than $4.50 a bushel. Wheat futures skyrocketed to near the unheard-of price of $6 a bushel.

"There is extraordinary volatility, and prices have gone up so fast that they can't sustain themselves," Glickman said.

Keith Collins, the USDA's chief economist, added: "The one thing you're concerned about in that situation is an overreaction. If you get prices way up to this unsustainable level, that causes people to behave in a certain way, it causes economic adjustments, and then if you get a crash. . . ."

Collins and Glickman know that many factors are contributing to the unusual situation: low stockpiles of grain, booming exports to other nations,

CHART 2   Corn

Futures contract on the Chicago Board of Trade, for delivery in May 1996.

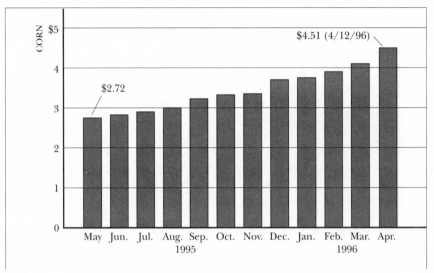

CHART 3   U.S. Food Prices

Meals at home and in restaurants, from the Consumer Price Index, seasonally adjusted (1982–1984 = 100).

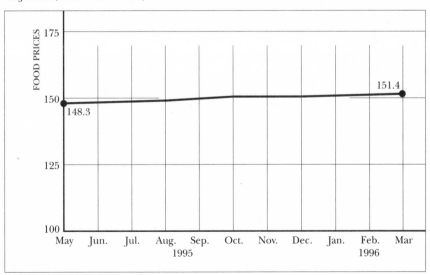

bad weather in wheat-growing regions such as Kansas, poor corn yields last year, large livestock herds, and new demand for corn products such as ethanol.

Moreover, the USDA on Thursday forecast that wheat supplies would hit 50-year lows before the spring harvest. The department also predicted the tightest corn supplies since the late 1930s.

Still, some of the factors driving prices up will change. If farmers have proven anything this century, it's an amazing ability to produce food. A new wheat crop will start filling the bins in May and June, and a new corn crop will follow in September and October. The USDA is hoping a bumper harvest will cool off the overheated markets—even Glickman, who would otherwise be rooting for crop prices to rise.

But until harvest begins, grain users are nervous. High feed prices are devastating to livestock producers. Until after the harvest, there's talk of spot shortages and scarcity.

"Basically, you can't buy a boatload of soft red wheat for April delivery because stocks are so tight," said Greg Doud, an analyst with U.S. Wheat Associates. "Hard red wheat is very, very close to that type of position. Soft winter wheat is also close to that position."

In keeping with the USDA's new philosophy, Glickman is letting the marketplace sort it out.

"We're not going to run out of grain," Glickman said. "The market rations that through price. Now, the question is, how high will the price go . . . before it begins to affect livestock herds, before it begins to affect consumption patterns?"

In the longer term, Glickman said, "there will be more acreage [planted], not only here but around the world, so at some point prices will come down. But I don't see a scenario very soon where we get back to $2 wheat. I think we're talking about stronger prices for a long time."

The 1996 Farm Bill*

NEW YORK TIMES

For months, Democrats objected that a Republican-led overhaul of America's farm programs, ending New Deal crop subsidies to farmers and replacing them with gradually declining flat payments over seven years, would shred a valuable Government safety net.

But after a House-Senate panel struck a deal on that very approach this week, President Clinton and senior Congressional Democrats bit their lips and reluctantly agreed to go along.

What happened?

First of all, Congress had to act. The five-year old law had expired, and everyone agreed that reverting to the permanent 1949 law was impractical and far too expensive. Most important, the new Republican majority was convinced that a change to free-market principles in farming was critical to keep the United States competitive in the world market. They also believed that the changes would eventually save money.

The timing was crucial. The nation's 1.5 million farmers were clamoring for a quick resolution because planting season has started in many areas. And no one wanted to alienate farmers in an election year.

But the apparent surrender by the Democrats could also be a tactical retreat. Lobbyists and members of Congress representing those with small farms, which are most vulnerable to market swings, are already regrouping

*This article, by Eric Schmitt, appeared in the *New York Times*, March 24, 1996.

to take another run at the farm bill next year. And if Mr. Clinton is re-elected this fall, he promises, he will lead the charge to protect farmers against natural disasters or price collapses.

"I am firmly committed to working with Congress next year to strengthen the farm safety net," Mr. Clinton said on Friday, "and I plan to propose legislation to do so."

Congress could not have picked a better time to retool the country's agricultural policy. Under the new approach, farmers are guaranteed $4 billion to $5 billion a year in transitional payments through 2002. At the same time, crop prices are at 10-year highs. So farmers win both ways.

"It's easier to look at change in times when you have better prices," said Bill Northey, president of the National Corn Growers Association, representing 30,000 farmers in 25 states, "but I don't think anyone believes that these better prices will be with us for the whole seven years."

That is what many Democrats fear. "When prices decline, and they will, thousands of farmers will be forced off their land," said Senator Kent Conrad, Democrat of North Dakota. "This will not only devastate farms, but also banks and Main Street businesses."

Free-market proponents acknowledge that the new approach carries more risk. But the tradeoff is that most government controls over planting decisions will end, letting farmers grow what they want to take advantage of export markets. Current controls affect only the farmers in the program; many others do not participate and have always been able to plant what they want.

Underlying this approach is the Republican goal of reducing Federal spending. Republicans say their bill will cost more initially than the current program but will save $2 billion over seven years. The bill follows trends in France and many other European countries, which have drastically pared farm subsidies.

"If you look at the big picture over the long term, this will require farmers to use their wits and tools of the marketplace more aggressively," Agriculture Secretary Dan Glickman said in an interview.

Agricultural economists say the new policy will mostly affect small and medium-sized farms, particularly in the Upper Midwest and Southwest, that grow crops covered by the Federal program, like wheat, rice, cotton and corn.

Mr. Glickman said the Administration wanted to develop more innovative "risk-management" mechanisms for farmers and would explore changes with private industry to the often-criticized crop insurance program. The House-Senate panel ended the requirement that farm-program participants buy crop insurance.

The Agriculture Department has started two pilot programs in Iowa and

Nebraska that would safeguard farmers against natural disasters and low market prices. Congressional experts are also looking at various tax-deferred financing mechanisms for farmers.

Democrats are expected to try again to eliminate a cap on the rates of loans that farmers can take out, using their crops as collateral.

The new approach, called Freedom to Farm by its supporters, would accelerate the ongoing consolidation of smaller, less profitable farms into larger, more efficient corporate farms. That has serious implications, not only for the face of farming in America but also for the livelihoods of rural communities.

"The ongoing trend is being driven by changes in technology and in agriculture," said Marvin Duncan, an agricultural economist at North Dakota State University. "Freedom to Farm tends to speed up that process. Whether that's good or bad depends on one's philosophical position."

Milking Pennsylvania Consumers*

PHILADELPHIA INQUIRER

S hoppers at Brown's Thriftway in Pennsauken can buy a gallon of whole milk for $1.99. If they cross the river and buy the same gallon in Pennsylvania, it will cost at least $2.43.

It is not a fluke.

Every day the same company that delivers thousands of half-pints of milk to the Philadelphia School District also delivers milk to the Palmyra School District in New Jersey. The crates, containers and milk are the same. There's one big difference: the price.

Last year alone, Philadelphia taxpayers spent $1 million more for school milk than if they had been charged prices available to New Jersey districts.

It wasn't corruption, inefficiency or improper billing that led to higher milk prices for consumers and schools. It was state law.

Pennsylvania is one of only three states that set minimum prices for the sale of milk to consumers. Milk prices are determined by the Pennsylvania Milk Marketing Board, an independent agency funded by the milk industry. It has been in existence since the mid-1930s, operating with state authority under a system that most states now consider antiquated, but that remains in Pennsylvania, Maine and North Dakota.

As many as 30 states, including New Jersey, once set minimum milk prices.

*This article, by Karl Stark, appeared in the *Philadelphia Inquirer*, April 14, 1996.

Pennsylvania is the only state that requires school districts to pay higher-than-market milk prices. So, in addition to inflating consumers' grocery bills, the system cost school taxpayers across Pennsylvania $10 million last year. That doesn't include higher milk prices for hospitals, prisons and college cafeterias. Retailers and wholesalers can be fined in Pennsylvania for selling milk below set prices.

Here are some other little-known details about the milk regulations:

The higher profits for the sale of milk in Pennsylvania don't go to farmers. The extra money goes mostly to middlemen—the people who process and deliver the milk—and to large supermarkets. Many large supermarket chains are exempted from Pennsylvania's minimum pricing when they buy milk. The reason, according to experts and federal court testimony, is that the board doesn't want large supermarket chains to buy cheaper milk in other states. Supermarkets in Pennsylvania could legally send their trucks out of state to bring in milk.

Still, consumers face the higher retail prices at Pennsylvania supermarkets. The result is milk is an unusually high profit item for many supermarkets in Pennsylvania.

The inflated cost of milk in Pennsylvania has contributed to higher milk prices at many supermarkets in South Jersey. Most out-of-state stores choose not to compete on milk prices to increase profits. Few people notice because most consumers do not look at the price when they buy milk, said Vin Samuel, dairy economist for the New Jersey Department of Agriculture.

Most consumers, Samuel said, value the convenience of buying their food all in one place. "When a consumer comes in to buy his groceries, generally he's not going to run around and price a gallon of milk," Samuel said. "He's going to get it at the same store."

Samuel added: "When you look at the price farmers are receiving, there's a large mark-up by the time it gets sold."

Although many supermarkets in New Jersey charge $2.54 and up for a gallon of whole milk, savvy shoppers can do better, typically at smaller markets or other outlets in New Jersey. For example, whole milk sells for $1.96 a gallon at Sam's Club in Delran. New Jersey law doesn't specify minimums, although it requires that stores sell milk at least 5 percent above cost.

"I choose to discount because the room's there," said Steve Brown, owner of Brown's Thriftway in Pennsauken, which sells a gallon of milk for $1.99.

STORES AND DEALERS WIN

The Pennsylvania Milk Marketing Board, whose three members set milk prices in six regions across the state, is supposed to arbitrate among dairy farmers, milk processors, sellers and consumers.

"The Pennsylvania Milk Marketing Board was supposedly set up for farmers and consumers. They're the two who get the least out of the board," said Harry Brownfield, who was the board's general counsel in 1994. "The two biggest beneficiaries now are milk dealers and the stores."

Pennsylvania's milk price system is so old that the Ridge administration looked at disbanding the Milk Board last year but backed off because of pending changes to federal agricultural rules.

"Now it's an appropriate time to revisit that," Russell C. Redding, a deputy secretary of the state Department of Agriculture, said of milk regulations.

Jerry Feaser, a spokesman for Ridge, said last week that the governor was considering eliminating the board.

"We don't want to just wholesale eliminate without reviewing it," Feaser said. "Gov. Ridge has demonstrated he's willing to end certain programs and even departments if he believes it is no longer a proper use of taxpayer money."

Donald A. Tortorice, a lawyer for the Pennsylvania Association of Milk Dealers, defended the Milk Board.

"There are isolated criticisms that can be made of any regulatory system," he said, "but this is one of the few that really work well."

He said the state legislature had allowed the Milk Board to continue because it helped maintain high milk quality and prevented prices from rising. He also said the board helped to support milk processors and distributors in Pennsylvania.

Pennsylvania officials began setting milk prices in 1934. The Pennsylvania Milk Marketing Board was created to guarantee a sufficient milk supply for Pennsylvania consumers and ensure that farmers were paid for their milk during the Depression.

Today, Pennsylvania is the fourth-largest dairy state in the country, and consumers have an abundant supply of milk. Most farmers in Pennsylvania, as in other producing states, are already protected by federal pricing regulations, which set wholesale milk prices for farmers.

Under the Milk Board rules, dairy farmers get a bonus—about 3 percent above the federal minimum price—if they sell milk within the state. About 25 percent of Pennsylvania farmers receive the bonus, according to Mel Eckhaus, dairy specialist of the Pennsylvania Farm Bureau.

The high retail prices set by the Milk Board create windfalls for dairy processors and retailers who by law can buy milk at the lowest price and sell it at the inflated levels set by the board.

"There is always this lip service paid to keeping the price of milk low," said Brownfield, the board's former general counsel. "Whenever we would have a price hearing and we would be playing with the statistics gathered at the hearing, trying to arrive at an acceptable price, the consumer's interest was the last thing that was thought about."

Marianne Olson, who served on the board from 1977 to 1983, said the board has no legitimate reason to exist.

"It hasn't been necessary for years," she said. "It isn't anything that anybody but the industry wants. It's just a secret little perk from the past that the milk industry has."

The Philadelphia School District has complained for years that it was being overcharged for milk. School officials say they have had to pay the higher prices, unlike some supermarket chains, because they lack clout with the Milk Board.

In a hearing requesting lower prices before the board last summer, the school district complained that it was paying more than 18 cents per half-pint when New Jersey firms said they were willing to supply milk for 5 cents less—a difference of $1 million a year.

However, the Milk Board prohibits Pennsylvania school districts from buying milk at lower prices.

As a result of the hearing, the school district won a 1¼-cent reduction per half-pint. The school district's lawyer, Eric B. Schnurer, appealed, arguing that prices remain 3½ cents too high. The school district also says the entire system is unconstitutional and is asking Commonwealth Court to eliminate it.

"It just seems there's a better place to put a million dollars each year than going into some milk processors' pockets," said Harold M. Harris Jr., an agricultural professor at Clemson University in South Carolina who testified for the school district. "It's going from poor school kids to quite-well-off businessmen. I don't think you have to be bleeding-heart liberal to agree that's a pretty bad welfare transfer."

Asked why the Philadelphia School District has to continue paying more than New Jersey districts, the Milk Board's executive secretary, O. Frank DeGarcia, said: "Don't you give me another state. I'm only concerned about the state of Pennsylvania. How they sell [in New Jersey] is their problem. Philadelphia wants to become another state? That's their problem. We have a system. They can follow the system."

NO APPEARANCE OF FAIRNESS

Even former board employees say that the board lacks a basic appearance of fairness. Board members are appointed by the governor, subject to approval by the legislature.

The board's $2.4 million annual budget is funded entirely by the state's dairy industry.

State law requires that at least one board member be designated to represent consumer interests. The board's consumer member, J. Robert Derry, is a retired dairy company executive.

Board member Beverly R. Minor and her husband own a dairy farm in Western Pennsylvania. Board chairman Leon H. Wilkinson is a retired dairy farmer whose four sons run a large dairy operation in Chester County.

"I milked a lot of cows in my life," Wilkinson said. "I can't go in there and look to the good of the farmer, which I'd like to, because all my four sons are farmers. I have to rule what the market allows."

CHART 1   Milk Prices

Some New Jersey milk prices, all whole milk, one gallon, compared to Pennsylvania state-regulated minimum price.

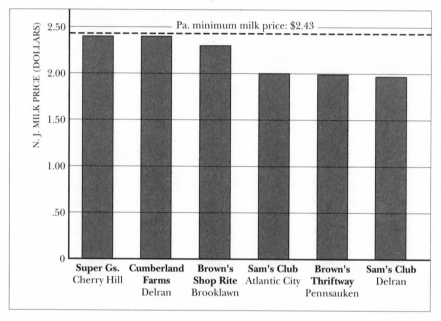

Source: *Philadelphia Inquirer* research.

All three members regularly make decisions that affect either their relatives' milk businesses or milk firms they worked for.

Brownfield, the board's former lawyer, said it was improper for board members to rule on prices that affect businesses with which they have been connected.

"To have a completely honest system, they should recuse themselves," he said.

Former board members say it is impossible for consumers to have an effective voice on the board.

Paul A. O'Hop Sr., the board's consumer member from 1983 to 1989, said he was usually powerless to reduce price requests from the industry. Noting that the other members at the time, Derry and Wilkinson, had connections to the dairy industry, O'Hop said: "What do you think the odds are of a consumer member swaying them, outside of sheer logic and forensic debate? There isn't a hell of a lot you can do. You can raise both hands and still get one vote."

Olson, the board's consumer member for six years, said: "The thing that really bothered me was the lack of fairness toward the public. The other members encouraged by the industry would never be willing to come up with a fair price. They always insisted on trying to pull things to inflate the base price. No one was allowed to see the books. Consumers never knew if the information was true or not."

Olson, who now lives in Wisconsin, was a Democratic Party worker in Pennsylvania when she served. Records show she frequently lost 2-1 votes on the board.

Derry, the board's current consumer member, could not be reached for comment.

LINKS TO INDUSTRY

The Milk Board's closeness to the milk industry is no secret. Earl B. Fink, now executive director of the Pennsylvania Association of Milk Dealers, was the board's executive secretary from 1977 to 1984. John C. Pierce, the board's secretary from 1985 to 1990, now works as general manager for Rosenberger's Dairies.

In addition, when the board wanted to update its computer system and software that helps set milk prices, it solicited a sole-source proposal from Herbein & Associates, whose principal, Carl Herbein, is the accountant of the milk dealers' association. "There just isn't anyone else that knows this industry in Pennsylvania," Herbein said in an interview.

Schnurer, the Philadelphia school district's milk lawyer, said he was not surprised.

"This confirms the general argument we've been making," he said. "There's a very cozy fraternal relationship between the dealers and the Milk Marketing Board."

QUESTIONS FOR ANALYSIS

1. In the spring of 1996, prices of corn and wheat were at record levels. Was this because of rightward shifts of the demand curves for corn and wheat?

2. Were the record prices of corn and wheat due to leftward shifts of the supply curves for corn and wheat?

3. According to the first article in the *Philadelphia Inquirer*, "High feed prices are devastating to livestock production." Why?

4. According to Senator Conrad of North Dakota, "When [farm] prices decline, and they will, thousands of farmers will be forced off their land." Do you agree? If so, is this bad for the country as a whole?

5. Why is milk an unusually high profit item in many Pennsylvania supermarkets?

6. Do you agree with Marianne Olson that the Pennsylvania Milk Marketing Board "hasn't been necessary for years." Why or why not?

7. Do you believe that Pennsylvania school districts should pay higher-than-market prices? Why or why not?

PART SEVEN

GDP AND ECONOMIC GROWTH

Policymakers have an obvious interest in promoting increases in gross domestic product. To understand what they are up to, you need to know what gross domestic product is. Robert Eisner of Northwestern University describes some of the limitations of existing measures. Edwin Mansfield of the University of Pennsylvania provides evidence that the social rate of return from investments in new technology has been relatively high. President Clinton's Council of Economic Advisers takes up the central question: How fast can the U.S. economy grow on a sustainable basis?

Some Limitations of the GDP Figures*

ROBERT EISNER

The critical definition of final product in the conventional accounts runs into some significant difficulties in its implications for government. Take state expenditures for road maintenance, for example. These outlays, to construction companies and maintenance crews, are by the official definition part of final product—purchases not resold. But is not the final product really the services of the roads, even though these are not generally purchased directly or sold?

Or take police services. Are they final product or are they intermediate product, essential to protecting businesses that produce the final product or to giving consumers a chance to enjoy it? The anomaly may be seen in noting what would happen to our measure of gross domestic product if General Motors were to work out an arrangement with the city of Flint, Michigan, to stop furnishing police protection for its plant in return for an abatement of its property taxes. General Motors would then use what it had paid in these indirect taxes to pay a private protection agency to guard its property. This agency would hire the police released by the city.

Government expenditures for goods and services would then be decreased by the amount of the police salaries. But the cost of producing the automobiles would be unchanged, because payments to the private protec-

*Robert Eisner is professor of economics at Northwestern University. This article comes from his *The Misunderstood Economy* (Cambridge: Harvard Business School, 1995).

tion agency would equal the "indirect business taxes" no longer paid. The value of the output of automobiles would be unchanged. Our measure of gross domestic product would be reduced by the amount of the police salaries, which had been the "final product" of government, even though the only change had been in who paid them—now business instead of government. What had been a final product purchased by government, final because it was paid for in taxes rather than sold, now became intermediate, the sale of services by the private protection agency to General Motors, which in turn resold them as part of its automobiles, which *were* final product.

The final-intermediate product issue turns in the opposite direction in the case of media services financed by advertising. The movie we see in a theater or rent from a video store is valued in final product as what we pay for it. But if we watch the same movie on commercial television, its expense turns up as a cost to the sponsor, a payment, say, by General Motors to ABC television. It is thus "intermediate" in the production and marketing of GM cars, adding nothing to their real value and hence nothing to gross domestic product.

With our conventional official accounts, therefore, gross domestic product goes down as people abandon movie theaters to watch films "for free" on their own TVs. But is their economic well-being really less? Then, if they subsequently abandon free television to subscribe to HBO or Cinemax or rent movies from their local video store, gross domestic product goes up.

Despite the definitions and focus on output for the market, the official accounts actually include a number of "imputations" for the value of output that is not sold in the market. Thus, they add the value of food and fuel produced and consumed on farms. They also include the value of "free" food and lodging provided by employers to employees, particularly domestic workers, and the value of financial services provided to consumers without charge or without charge of full cost, such as free checking services given to depositors in lieu of paying them some or all of the interest earned on their deposits.

Most important, they include the rental values of owner-occupied dwellings. Without this imputation the gross domestic product would go down dramatically as Americans increasingly abandoned the rental market, where the rents they paid were a measure of the housing services in the GDP, to buy new houses or condominiums, where the owners in a sense paid rent to themselves rather than in a market transaction. In effect, the accounts make believe that homeowners are in business. Their business is that of being landlords, who rent to themselves. It is thus that purchases of new houses by these homeowner-businesses are counted as investment, just as is the purchase of a new building by any other business.

Once we admit the need for imputations of some nonmarket production we open up a whole Pandora's Box. There are vast additional amounts of vital services produced by men and, particularly, women in the home, which are not destined for sale in the market. Virtually all of the services of government—whether we like them or not and whether they are paid for by taxes or borrowing—are provided to the public without charge, that is, without market transactions. And we must make many other extensions and revisions of the conventional accounts before we are able to fully measure economic contributions to our well-being, or the effects of debt and deficits on those contributions.

EXTENDED AND REVISED NATIONAL INCOME ACCOUNTS

Consider the old anecdote about the Yuppie who uses some of *his* (note the sexism) high income to hire a housekeeper. He pays *her,* say, $20,000 a year out of his $80,000 salary to keep his luxury apartment in order, to do the marketing and cooking, and generally offer all the comforts he had come to expect from dear old Mom. The Bureau of Economic Analysis, if it included the Yuppie and his housekeeper in its numbers, would find $100,000 of income going into national income. This would correspond to $100,000 of the gross domestic product that they were paid to produce— the $80,000 of advice that the Yuppie gave to clients of his brokerage firm and the $20,000 of housekeeping services produced by the housekeeper.

But suppose that the relationship between the Yuppie and his housekeeper deepens. They fall in love and marry. Our Yuppie now devotes $20,000 a year to meet his wife's personal expenses, which she had previously paid out of her $20,000 salary. What happens to national income and gross domestic product? The BEA will now find the couple earning only $80,000 of national income and contributing only $80,000 to the gross domestic product. While the same services are now being performed—perhaps, with the stimulus of love, more—the national income and product have declined. Activities that entailed "market" transactions are no longer counted because they have become "nonmarket."

HOUSEHOLD WORK AND OTHER NONMARKET ACTIVITY

The story, apocryphal and unrealistic as it may be—it ignores tax considerations, for example—illustrates a vitally important point. Our official conventional accounts omit vast amounts of nonmarket output, particularly within the household. My own conservative estimates suggest that including the value of unpaid labor services in the home would have increased our 1992 gross domestic product of $6 trillion by fully one-third. Think of all the activities we are not counting: child care, cooking, laundering, cleaning, marketing, entertaining—not to mention the value of connubial bliss, which would, if paid for in the market, probably be excluded as illegal, or unobserved, underground activity.

What makes the exclusion of nonmarket activities especially bothersome for serious economic analysis is that they are not a constant proportion of the market activities that are included. Over the past 200 years the economy of the United States has changed from one in which the great bulk of economic activity was nonmarket, e.g., making yarn at the old spinning wheel in the parlor, or growing crops on the frontier farm. Clothes are now store-bought and food comes packaged and even precooked. The bulk of production is sold and bought in the market. The growth in the market economy reflected in the official measures of gross domestic product and national income thus exceeds the growth in the entire U.S. economy, market and nonmarket.

If we compare the United States with less developed countries in Asia or Africa or Latin America, we find that their market economies are much smaller than ours but that the proportion of their output produced outside of the market is much greater. The people of India do not buy many TV dinners. They and the people of other less developed countries are indeed impoverished, but many of them at least are not starving, as they would be if their sustenance were limited to what they could purchase with their few hundred dollars per capita income. Thus, focus on the essentially market activities of the official or conventional accounts tends to exaggerate the long-run growth in developed countries and exaggerates the differences in living standards, though great in any event, between less developed and fully developed economies.

Omission of nonmarket activity from our accounts seriously distorts our measures of a most profound change in the U.S. economy over the past half-century: the massive movement of women into the labor force. Before World War II most women worked in market activities, if at all, until they had children (generally at an early age) and perhaps again after children were grown. Now, most women work for wages and salaries.

The movement of large numbers of women into the labor force has greatly increased market output. But has it increased total output as much? If paid child care is substituted for care by the mother in the home, is that a net increase in child care or output? If restaurant meals are substituted for home cooking, is that an increase in product? If women use part of their market income for commuting expenses, does all of their income properly reflect a net increase in well-being or in output?

Social Rates of
Return from R&D*

EDWIN MANSFIELD

B y a social rate of return, we mean the interest rate received by society as a whole from an investment. To economists, the social rate of return from investments in new technology is important, since it measures the payoff to society from these investments. A high social rate of return indicates that society's resources are being employed effectively and that more resources should be devoted to such investments if the rate of return stays high. In a series of papers, I have tried to describe the many difficulties in measuring and interpreting the social rate of return. They are numerous and important, but until something better comes along, estimates of this sort are likely to continue to be used.

Although earlier efforts to measure the social rates of return from such investments had been made in agriculture, the first attempt to measure the social rate of return from investments in industrial innovations was published in 1977. The innovations that were included in the study took place in a variety of industries, including primary metals, machine tools, industrial controls, construction, drilling, paper, thread, heating equipment, electronics, chemicals, and household cleaners. They occurred in firms of quite different sizes. Most of them were of average or routine importance,

*Edwin Mansfield is professor of economics at the University of Pennsylvania. This is an excerpt from his paper in *Technology, R&D, and the Economy* (Washington, D.C.: Brookings Institution, 1996).

TABLE 1   Social and Private Rates of Return from Investment in Seventeen Innovations

INNOVATION	RATE OF RETURN (PERCENT)	
	SOCIAL	PRIVATE
Primary metals innovation	17	18
Machine tool innovation	83	35
Component for control system	29	7
Construction material	96	9
Drilling material	54	16
Drafting innovation	92	47
Paper innovation	82	42
Thread innovation	307	27
Door-control innovation	27	37
New electronic device	Negative	Negative
Chemical product innovation	71	9
Chemical process innovation	32	25
Chemical process innovation	13	4
Major chemical process innovation	56	31
Household cleaning device	209	214
Stain remover	116	4
Dishwashing liquid	45	46
Median	56	25

not major breakthroughs. Although the sample could not be viewed as randomly chosen, there was no obvious sign that it was biased toward very profitable innovations (socially or privately) or relatively unprofitable ones. The findings (in Table 1) indicated that the median social rate of return from the investment in these innovations was 56 percent, a very high figure.

To extend this sample and replicate the analysis, the National Science Foundation commissioned two studies, one by Robert R. Nathan Associates and one by Foster Associates. Their results, like those in Table 1, indicate that the median social rate of return tends to be very high. On the basis of its sample of twenty innovations, Nathan Associates found the median social rate of return to be 70 percent. Foster Associates, on the basis of its sample of twenty innovations, found the median social rate of return to be 99 percent.

More recently, Manuel Trajtenberg estimated that the social rate of return to R&D in the field of CT scanners in medical technology was about 270 percent. As he is careful to point out, the interpretation of the gains as social depends on the motives underlying the behavior of hospitals when choosing medical technologies. Also, like hybrid corn, which Zvi Griliches studied, the rate of return would be expected to be high because the innovation was known in advance to be a gusher, not a dry hole. But bearing these things in mind, his results certainly are consistent with the proposition that the social rate of return from investments in new technology tends to be high.

SOCIAL VERSUS PRIVATE RATES OF RETURN

Although the social returns from innovative activities seem to be very high, this does not mean that the private returns—the returns to the innovating firm—are high. In Mansfield et al., whereas the median social rate of return was 56 percent, the median private rate of return was only 25 percent (see Table 1). Also, very rich and detailed data were obtained regarding the return from the innovative activities (in 1960 to 1972) of one of the country's biggest firms. For each year, this firm made a careful inventory of the technological innovations stemming from its R&D and related activities, and it made detailed estimates of the effect of each of these innovations on its profit stream. The average private rate of return from this firm's total investment in innovative activities was about 19 percent, which was much less than the social rate of return.

To understand why the private rate of return from innovative activity is so much lower than the social rate of return, it is important to recognize that the innovator often finds it very hard to appropriate the returns from the innovation. Many of these benefits accrue to imitators, who often obtain information quickly concerning the detailed nature and operation of the new products and processes developed by a firm. According to a study of 100 U.S. firms, this information is in the hands of at least some of their rivals within about a year, on the average, after a new product is developed. For processes, this information leaks out more slowly, but even in the case of processes, it generally leaks out in less than about fifteen months. The major exception is chemical processes, which often can be kept secret for a number of years.

CONCLUSIONS

Practically all the available evidence indicates that the economic payoff to society as a whole from investments in new technology has been very high, the average social rate of return being about 50 percent. There is no assurance that this very high rate of return will be maintained as more and more such investments are made, but thus far there is no convincing evidence that the marginal social rate of return has fallen substantially.

The economic payoff to the innovator is frequently much lower than to society as a whole. Information concerning a new technology leaks out more quickly than is generally recognized. In other than a few areas like pharmaceuticals and agricultural chemicals, the patent system frequently has only a limited effect on the rate of imitation. For investments from which the private rate of return in new technology is low (even though the social rate of return is relatively high), a case may be made for public support.

How Fast Can the U.S. Economy Grow?*

PRESIDENT CLINTON'S COUNCIL OF ECONOMIC ADVISERS

How fast can the economy grow on a sustainable basis? Most mainstream analysts currently believe that aggregate output can grow about 2.5 percent per year. Recently, however, some analysts—perhaps inspired by the outstanding performance of the economy in 1994—have asserted that much more rapid growth, possibly as fast as 5 percent per year, may be sustainable.

The answer to this question has profound implications for the future well-being of the American people. If the mainstream view is correct, aggregate output will double only every 28 years or so, and per capita output only about every 56 years (assuming population growth of 1 percent per year). But if the alternative view is correct, aggregate output could double every 14 years, and per capita output every 18 years.

The answer also has important implications for the conduct of government policy. Sensible Federal budget planning can proceed only in the context of a realistic assessment of the long-term outlook for the economy. If the outlook is robust, then a more expansionary fiscal policy may well be consistent with a responsible outcome on the deficit. If, on the other hand, the outlook is more subdued, a greater degree of fiscal restraint may be required.

*This is an excerpt from the *Economic Report of the President* (Washington, D.C.: Government Printing Office, 1995).

Chart 1 illustrates one simple method for assessing the sustainable rate of growth of gross domestic product (GDP). . . . The chart focuses on the growth of real GDP between the first quarter of 1988 and the fourth quarter of 1994. The reason for focusing on these two quarters is that the unemployment rate was very similar in both: 5.7 percent and 5.6 percent, respectively. This suggests that a similar fraction of the economy's overall productive capacity was being utilized in both quarters. Thus the average rate of growth of output in the interval between them should give a good indication of the average rate of growth of the economy's productive capacity during that period.

As the chart shows, real GDP increased at an average annual rate of 2.1 percent between the first quarter of 1988 and the fourth quarter of 1994. This suggests that the economy's productive capacity—potential GDP—also grew at about that rate. Over the same period, real GDP measured on the more conventional basis (1987 dollars) increased at an average annual rate of 2.3 percent. Therefore, this simple method suggests that the con-

CHART 1   Real Gross Domestic Product

Between the beginning of 1988 and the end of 1994, real GDP increased at an average annual rate of 2.1 percent.

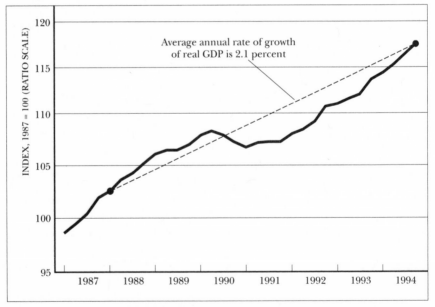

Note: Data are based on a chain-weighted measure.

Source: Department of Commerce.

sensus view that the sustainable rate of growth is about 2½ percent per year is slightly more optimistic than a purely mechanical reading of recent experience would warrant. . . .

FACTORS GENERATING GROWTH OF POTENTIAL GDP

Between 1963 and 1994 real U.S. GDP increased at an average annual rate of 3.1 percent per year. Because the economy appears to have been operating about at its potential in both those years, the average rate of growth of *actual* output between those dates should provide a relatively accurate estimate of the average rate of growth of *potential* output during the same period.

Growth of real GDP can be decomposed into two main components: growth of output per hour worked (or productivity) and growth of hours worked. As Chart 2 illustrates, these two components each contributed 1.7 percentage points to the growth of GDP between 1963 and 1994. (Strictly speaking, the data on productivity and hours worked pertain only to the private nonfarm business sector, whereas the data on output pertain to the

CHART 2   Factors Generating Growth of Gross Domestic Product

Since 1972, real GDP has increased more slowly than before, owing to a reduction in the rate of growth of output per hour worked.

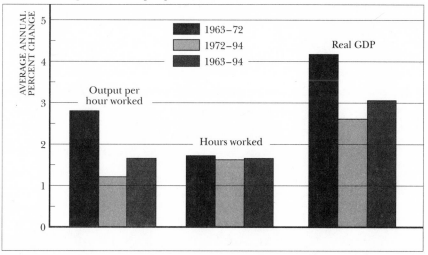

Note: Estimates of growth in output and output per hour are based on chain-weighted measures. Data on output per hour and hours worked pertain to the private nonfarm business sector, whereas the data on GDP pertain to the whole economy.

Sources: Council of Economic Advisers, Department of Commerce, and Department of Labor.

total economy. As a result, and because the output of the private nonfarm business sector was increasing slightly more rapidly than the output of the total economy, the growth of output per hour and the growth of hours worked add up to slightly more than the growth of GDP).

Chart 2 also shows that the average experience since 1963 subsumes two very different episodes. Between 1963 and 1972 real GDP increased at an average annual rate of 4.2 percent. By contrast, since 1972 real GDP has increased only about 2.6 percent per year. (The economy appears to have been operating at about its potential in 1972; as a result, that year should also serve as a useful benchmark for purposes of estimating potential GDP growth rates.) The slower rate of growth of GDP since 1972 can be attributed to a slowdown in the rate of growth of productivity, since the growth of hours worked was about as rapid after 1972 as before.

Chart 3 examines the slowdown in the growth of productivity in more detail. The chart illustrates one of the most significant economic developments of the postwar period. Whereas productivity in the private nonfarm

CHART 3 Output per Hour in the Private Nonfarm Business Sector

Productivity growth in the private nonfarm business sector seems to have slowed markedly sometime in the early 1970s.

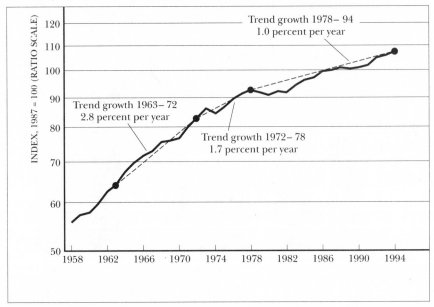

Note: Data are based on a chain-weighted measure.

Sources: Council of Economic Advisers and Department of Labor.

business sector increased at an average annual rate of 2.8 percent between 1963 and 1972, it increased only 1.7 percent per year between 1972 and 1978, and only 1.0 percent after 1978 (yet another year in which the economy was operating close to potential).

By contrast, productivity growth in the manufacturing sector seems to have slowed much less during the past four decades. As Chart 4 shows, output per hour in the manufacturing sector is estimated to have increased on average about 3.3 percent per year between 1963 and 1972, 2.6 percent between 1972 and 1978, and 2.6 percent again between 1978 and 1987. . . .

Taken together, Charts 3 and 4 suggest that the slowdown in the growth of productivity after 1972 was concentrated outside the manufacturing sector. It has been argued that these and similar data exaggerate that concentration, because they do not control for the fact that the manufacturing sector may have increasingly "outsourced" some low-productivity activities. For example, if factories contract with security firms to do work formerly done by their own security guards, that activity will be counted in the services rather than the manufacturing sector, and if security guards'

CHART 4　Output per Hour in the Manufacturing Sector

Productivity growth in the manufacturing sector appears to have slowed only a little since the 1960s and early 1970s.

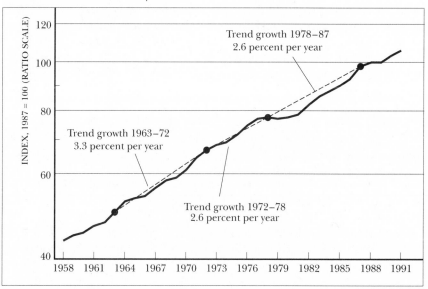

Note: Data are based on a chain-weighted measure.

Source: Department of Labor.

productivity is less than that of the factories' assembly-line workers, official statistics may report an increase in overall manufacturing productivity that does not reflect an increase in the productivity of any individual worker. What this argument ignores, however, is that *high*-productivity jobs may also have been outsourced, in which case the direction of bias in the official estimates would be ambiguous. On balance, the evidence suggests that the apparent strength of productivity growth in manufacturing is not a figment of job migration.

Much of the discussion in this chapter focuses on the slow rate of growth of productivity in the United States since the early 1970s, relative to earlier U.S. experience and the experience of other countries. But it is worth noting that U.S. workers remain among the most productive in the world. This suggests that the productivity "problem" in the United States has much more to do with the rate of growth of productivity than with its level. . . .

HAS THE TREND IN PRODUCTIVITY GROWTH IMPROVED RECENTLY?

Since 1987, according to current estimates, productivity growth in the private nonfarm business sector has averaged 1.2 percent per year, somewhat faster than the average during the previous decade. And since 1991, productivity growth has averaged about 2.0 percent per year—more than twice the 1978–87 average. Are recent claims of a pickup in trend productivity growth justified? (Provided there has been no offsetting reduction in the growth of hours, such a pickup would translate into an increase in the economy's potential growth rate.) This question is not easily resolved because the recent behavior of productivity has been heavily influenced (for the better) by the faster pace of economic activity during the last 2 years. A proper assessment of the trend in productivity growth can be made only by abstracting from cyclical influences.

Chart 5 focuses on the behavior of productivity since 1976. Between 1978 and 1982—a period that included the deepest recession of the postwar period—productivity actually declined slightly according to official estimates. Then, as recovery took hold, productivity rebounded. By 1987 the economy once again was operating in the neighborhood of its full potential. Between 1978 and 1987 the growth of productivity averaged about 0.9 percent per year.

Since 1987 this chain of events has essentially repeated itself: a period of slow growth in productivity as the economy endured a recession, followed by a period of rebound as the recovery gathered strength. Today, well into the expansion, the economy once again appears to be operating in the neighborhood of its potential. Between 1987 and 1994—as was noted above—productivity growth averaged about 1.2 percent per year. Thus,

CHART 5   Output per Hour in the Private Nonfarm Business Sector

Productivity has increased rapidly since 1991. Nonetheless, it is still difficult to know whether there has been an improvement in the trend rate of productivity growth.

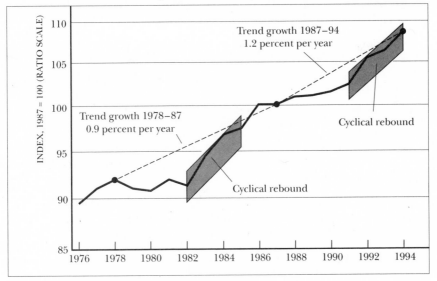

Note: Data are based on a chain-weighted measure.

Sources: Council of Economic Advisers and Department of Labor.

currently available data do seem to hint that the trend in productivity growth has picked up in the last few years. However, the magnitude of that pickup pales in comparison to the decline that occurred earlier in the post-war period. Moreover, the evidence in support of a pickup is still inconclusive. For example, if trends are computed for the periods 1978–86 and 1986–94 rather than 1978–87 and 1987–94, the suggestion of a pickup is much weaker: productivity growth averaged 1.0 percent per year in the earlier alternative subperiod and 1.1 percent in the later one. On the other hand, if the breakpoint chosen is 1988 or, especially, 1989, the evidence in favor of a pickup appears stronger. However, the averages over these later periods, especially the one since 1989, are dominated by the cyclical recovery and so may create a false impression of an improvement in the trend.

Furthermore, the Labor Department released data in 1994 suggesting that the growth of hours worked between 1993 and 1994 may be revised upward by enough to shave 0.1 percentage point off the average rate of productivity increase for the period 1987–94. Thus, while the evidence in favor of a slight improvement in the productivity growth trend is encouraging, it is not yet decisive. The experience of the next few years will be quite telling for this issue.

QUESTIONS FOR ANALYSIS

1. Are police services a final product or an intermediate product?

2. Why does GDP go down as people abandon movie theaters to watch films "for free" on their own TVs?

3. According to Eisner, "our official conventional accounts omit vast amounts of nonmarket output, particularly within the household." Give examples.

4. What is a social rate of return?

5. Why is the economic payoff to an innovator frequently much lower than to society as a whole?

6. President Clinton's Council of Economic Advisers is concerned with the question: How fast can the economy grow on a sustainable basis? Why is this question of fundamental importance?

7. The council suggests that "the productivity 'problem' in the United States has much more to do with the rate of growth of productivity than with its level." What does it mean?

8. Does the available evidence indicate that the trend in productivity growth has improved since the late 1980s?

9. Would you favor public policies designed to increase the rate of productivity growth in the United States? Why or why not?

PART EIGHT

FISCAL POLICY

Everyone who reads a newspaper or watches television must be aware that the United States is running a very large budget deficit. In the first article, John Kasich, who has been the head of the House Budget Committee, describes the problem as he sees it. Peter Peterson, chairman of the Blackstone Group and former secretary of commerce, argues that entitlements programs like Social Security and Medicare must be cut back, and that the middle class must be prepared for sacrifices. The third article shows how one newspaper—the *Philadelphia Inquirer*—would cut government spending.

The People's Budget*

JOHN KASICH

Entitlement programs like Medicare and Medicaid are growing at 10 percent every year; discretionary spending—supposedly limited by "spending caps" enacted in 1990—is growing almost as fast. Literally hundreds of agencies and programs are scattered through the government that simply don't work. And when you add it all up, you have deficits year after year, deficits that have accumulated in a federal debt of nearly $5 trillion.

That debt is one of the reasons change has to occur and has to occur immediately. According to the Joint Economic Committee, a child born in 1995 will pay $187,150 *just in interest payments* on the national debt. Our children will have fewer jobs, pay higher taxes, have lower incomes, and be less able to afford homes because of the debt. By raising interest rates and discouraging investment, the debt is slowing—some would say crippling—our ability to transition into the Information Age economy of the twenty-first century.

The path we are on today is one of slow but certain erosion of America's economic strength. No economy, no matter how prosperous, can afford to pile up literally trillions upon trillions of dollars of debt.

The path we are on today is also fundamentally wrong. It used to be that parents worked hard to pay off the mortgage so they could leave the house to their children. Today, it seems, we are selling off the house and leaving

*This is an excerpt from Edwin Dale, Jeffrey Eisenach, Frank Luntz, Timothy Muris, and William Schneider, *The People's Budget* (Washington, D.C.: Regnery Publishing, 1995).

the children with the mortgage. Balancing the budget is not just an economic issue. It is a moral imperative.

But the budget fight is ultimately about much more than the federal debt. It is about what kind of government we want to have in America. For the last forty years, government has taken power away from the people. The tax burden on the average American family—after adjusting for inflation—has nearly tripled, from $6,970 in 1959 to $18,500 in 1995. Fully half of the average family's income now goes to pay taxes to federal, state, and local governments combined. As the government's budget has grown, the people's budget has shrunk.

Every time government takes a dollar from an American family, it is a dollar less that the family has to spend on feeding, educating, providing health care, and creating a safe and nurturing home for its children. It is a dollar less it has to provide for the parents' retirement or to help out grandparents.

For forty years, the government in Washington has acted as though it, not the American people, was responsible for these things. It has taken money from people to create centralized, bureaucratic programs, run by well-meaning government employees who are asked to do the impossible: design a "one-size-fits-all" government for a country of 260 million people. The simple reality is that it doesn't work and it can't work. It is a matter of common sense: no one can sit in Washington, D.C. and try to tell people in Columbus, Ohio; Austin, Texas; Abilene, Kansas; New York, New York; Detroit, Michigan; and Los Angeles, California the best way to educate children, house the poor, build the roads, and do the literally thousands of other things now dictated from Washington.

The new majority in the House will produce a budget to completely transform the government in Washington. . . . We will:

□ end the myth of federal compassion by sending responsibility for welfare programs back to the states, the localities, and the people;

□ reform the Pentagon to make it more efficient, and revitalize America's defenses and cut foreign aid;

□ cut subsidies to the hundreds of special interests—the privileged, the powerful, and the elite—who have fed for too long at the federal trough;

□ send control over dozens of government activities back to the states, restoring the spirit of the Tenth Amendment of the Constitution;

□ and save the Medicare system from bankruptcy by transforming it into a 21st century system of consumer choice and quality health care.

And when we are done we will have a smaller government, lower taxes, and a balanced budget.

The Third Rail of American Politics*

PETER PETERSON

Ican't remember who it was who first said that you could take all the economists in the world, lay them end to end—and still not reach a conclusion. But if you listen carefully to most economists and policy experts today, there is actually a great deal of consensus about the magnitude of America's economic challenges and what sorts of reforms will be necessary to overcome them.

In particular, most would agree to the following: (1) To get American living standards rising again, we must increase productivity. (2) To boost productivity we must invest more—much, much more—not just in machines, but in R&D, in infrastructure, and in people. Many, myself included, think that *at least $400 billion a year in new investments are needed.* (3) This in turn means we must save much, much more—*$400 billion a year more.* (4) The surest and fastest way to increase our savings is to reduce and eventually eliminate the federal deficit, which is really just a form of "negative" public savings. (5) To reduce the deficit and keep it down we must make major cuts in consumption spending, and in particular in entitlements. But this, alas, requires us to confront a brute question: If we are to save more by consuming less, *whose* consumption growth do we propose to cut?

It's at this point that agreement on what needs to be done—while not ex-

*This is an excerpt from Peter Peterson, *Facing Up* (New York: Simon and Schuster, 1994). Peter Peterson is chairman of the Blackstone Group and a former secretary of commerce.

actly breaking down—comes face-to-face with a truth that remains politically inexpressible. That truth is that the problem is all of us. *Most Americans—emphatically including the middle class—will have to give something up, at
least temporarily, to get back our American Dream.*

We all remember Bill Clinton's damning campaign slogan: "It's the
economy, stupid." Well, when it comes to the budget the watchword ought
to be "It's entitlements, stupid." From Social Security and Medicare to farm
aid and federal pensions, it is these benefit programs that dominate the
budget today. In 1993, entitlement outlays totaled a staggering $761 bil-
lion—or 54 percent of all federal spending. And that doesn't include $150
billion more in back-door benefits passed out through the tax code, such as
the deduction for home mortgage interest and the exclusion from taxable
income of employer-paid health care. (These subsidies, which are the fiscal
equivalent of a check in the mail, are technically called "tax expenditures.")

CHART 1   Federal Spending by Major Budget Functions and Federal
Deficit

Entitlement spending dominates the federal budget.

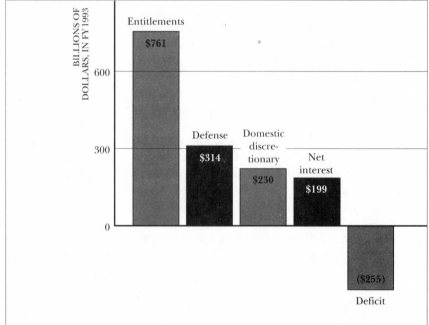

Note: Budget functions are defined by the Congressional Budget Office. Defense includes
"International" discretionary spending.

It is the explosive growth in entitlements, moreover, that threatens to rob our future. I've already noted that even with the Clinton deficit reduction package in place, entitlement outlays are slated to grow by $393 billion in today's dollars between 1994 and 2004. This means that, along with interest costs, they will account for all growth in federal spending over the next decade. In fact, apart from entitlements and net interest, other federal outlays are actually scheduled to decline by $31 billion in real terms between 1994 and 2004. If this seems surprising, recall that the President is aggressively clipping the Pentagon's wings—so that by 1998 we will be spending less on defense, as a share of GDP, than in any year since Pearl Harbor. As for future domestic discretionary spending—for everything from R&D and space exploration to immigration control and law enforcement—this too is expected to shrink as a share of GDP, and by 1997 will have sunk back beneath the postwar record low it reached late in the Reagan administration.

The usual solutions no longer apply. Even if we immediately and permanently cut defense spending by half, twenty years from now we would again

CHART 2 Projected Changes in Federal Spending from FY 1994 to FY 2004 by Major Budget Function

Along with interest payments, entitlements will account for all real federal spending growth over the next decade.

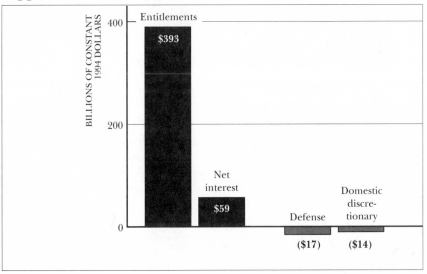

Note: Budget projections by the Congressional Budget Office. Defense includes "International" discretionary spending.

face the same deficit burden as today. We can keep raising tax rates, but to keep up with the growth of entitlements alone we would have to enact a new tax hike, equal to the one sponsored by President Clinton, roughly every four years for the next half century. What we must now confront is the need to cut entitlements.

President Clinton, it's true, never promised to leave all entitlements untouched. But he did make a sweeping social promise that was just as unfortunate in its effects. He assured the public that nothing in his budget would take much away from any household belonging to the "middle class." According to Clinton's definition, moreover, only about 1 percent of all U.S. tax filers—for example, joint-filing couples with gross incomes over $200,000—are too rich to be included in the middle class.

As a guide to tax reform, Clinton's promise was unfortunate enough. Americans with incomes over $200,000 earn just 13 percent of all pretax income in the United States. It shouldn't take any arcane knowledge of fiscal arithmetic to see that balancing the budget on such a narrow stretch of income territory is quite literally impossible. In fact, if President Clinton had wanted to balance the budget by taxing the "rich" alone, he would have had to tax away *all* the taxable income of everyone with more than $175,000 of gross income. Or, taking a less draconian approach, he might merely have *doubled* the income taxes of the "affluent"—but that would have required including everyone down to about $50,000 of income. Even this kinder and gentler approach would amount to something like expropriation—hardly the kind of policy consistent with either free markets or democracy.

But Clinton's promise to the middle class was most damaging in its impact on entitlement reform, since it precluded major savings from the largest and fastest growing part of the budget. Households with incomes over $200,000 received just 1 percent ($5 billion) of federal entitlement outlays in 1991. No one is—or should be—talking about significant entitlement cuts for lower-income Americans. That leaves all households with incomes above the U.S. household median—roughly $30,000 in 1991—yet below $200,000, in other words, that part of Clinton's "middle class," which, however hard-pressed, cannot claim to be destitute.

In 1991, such households received no less than 43 percent of all benefit dollars ($227 billion) disbursed under major Federal entitlement programs. It is worth noting, moreover, that this absolute dollar figure almost certainly understates the total benefit dollars going to the $30,000 to $200,000 income bracket, since it only reflects the 80 percent of entitlement outlays flowing through programs for which we have accurate income data on recipients. What about the remaining 20 percent? We cannot be sure. Some of it flows through programs such as Medicaid, which mostly benefit lower-income households; some too flows through programs such as student loans, farm aid, and veterans' health care, which disproportionately benefit upper-income households. All told, it would be safe to assume that total federal benefit outlays reaching the $30,000 to $200,000 income bracket amounted to at least $265 billion in 1991.

Then consider our ocean of so-called tax expenditures—the subtle subsidies that help Americans borrow huge sums for home mortgages and that underwrite gold-plated employer health plans. Here the share received by Clinton's "middle-class" is larger still. Over two-thirds go to tax filers with incomes between $30,000 and $200,000. Just 7 percent go to the Americans whom the President calls "rich."

The lesson in these numbers seems clear. Any plan to balance the budget that exempts the broad middle class from sacrifice is doomed to failure. But if we are willing to ask for even modest sacrifices from all Americans with incomes above about $30,000, the picture changes entirely. Suddenly we're talking about a whopping 73 percent of national household income. We're also talking about a stunning 74 percent of all tax expenditures and 43 percent of federal entitlement outlays. Taken together, these benefits amounted to $372 billion in 1991. That's a sum that we simply cannot ignore if we are at all serious about putting our fiscal house in order.

Let's pause for a moment to ask ourselves: What in reality is the "middle class"? Ask any American if he or she is "middle class," and the answer will almost always be "yes!" The truly poor will admit to being "lower middle class" and the rich will go along with "upper middle class," but few will forthrightly call themselves "poor" or "rich." This is a characteristically American self-perception, and it reflects our desire to live in a basically egalitarian society. Next, ask any group of Americans to specify the annual income that defines "middle class" and you'll hear responses ranging from, say, $20,000 all the way up to $200,000—if we include the Clinton administration's definition.

But there are more precise and realistic definitions. The median U.S. household income in 1993 (including nontaxable government and employer benefits) was $31,700. If you narrowly define middle class to comprise one-half of all American households, equally distributed around that $31,700 household, the statistical middle-class income turns out to range from $14,040 to $55,880.

This exposition regularly startles those who are new to it. A household with $60,000 of income invariably thinks of itself as "just getting by," but it actually stands in the top quarter of U.S. households. A two-earner couple with an income totaling $120,000 may think of itself as just middle class. In fact, that two-earner couple stands in the top 5 percent of American households. By the time we reach those with incomes in excess of $200,000, we are left with a mere statistical sliver of the population: roughly 1 percent.

Middle-class Americans today, it seems, suffer from what might be called a "reverse Lake Wobegon" syndrome. As Garrison Keillor fans know, Lake Wobegon is a wonderful fictional place where all the children are *above* average. When it comes to incomes, however, most middle-class Americans, trying hard to make ends meet, assume they must be *below* average.

The broad middle class likes to think that because they aren't genuinely rich, they can't possibly be part of the solution to America's economic problems, and that because they aren't truly poor (aren't a dysfunctional family on welfare, for example), they can't possibly be part of the problem itself. Both lines of reasoning are fallacious. As the accompanying charts show, a huge share of the escalating budget for federal benefit programs is not spent on welfare for the poor, as is commonly thought, but on subsidizing the broad middle class. The truth is that middle-income Americans, just like all other Americans, are on the dole—the entitlement dole. But few realize it. Facing up means facing the fact that we are *all* on welfare of one kind or another.

When middle-class benefits come in the form of Social Security and Medicare payments, or military and civil service pensions, they don't seem like *subsidies* in the sense that welfare checks to the poor are. "I've worked hard all my life; I'm just getting what I am entitled to," middle-class retirees say. And there's exactly the problem! . . . [A]*ll of us* have decided that we are *entitled* to much more than our society can afford to pay for—especially if we want to find the means to invest in our children and our collective future.

A Better Balance*

PHILADELPHIA INQUIRER

*F*ive trillion dollars. That's what the national debt will reach this year. It means $19,000 in IOUs for every man, woman and child in America. For young people, this reckless borrowing is especially unfair because they will live the longest with its consequences.

Last month, President Clinton proposed a five-year plan for piling another $1 trillion on top of this debt. He calls his plan for continued deficit spending "controlling" the problem. We call it irresponsible. It burdens the economy; it cheats children.

For their part, Republicans in the House say they want spending cuts, but so far they have zeroed in on the poor and disadvantaged.

Clearly, the federal government must do better at reducing waste and fraud in safety-net programs such as food stamps and the working-poor tax credit. But a farsighted Congress would re-invest such savings into job-oriented welfare reform.

The spending-cut plan that the House Budget Committee passed last week avoids specifics, treads lightly on entitlements, and most of its savings would go toward cutting taxes—not the deficit.

The best way to put the U.S. economy on a sound footing is to stop massive borrowing that drains hundreds of billions in savings out of the private sector. Yet the Clinton budget for next year has the deficit at $196.7 billion and rising.

*This editorial appeared in the *Philadelphia Inquirer* on March 19, 1995.

Instead, the deficit ought to be *$50 billion–$60 billion lower* than he proposed. If that pace of deficit reduction were continued for four years, the budget would be balanced in 1999.

Here is a plan to slash the deficit in fiscal 1996, which starts in October. This *understates* what can be done because it doesn't include anything worth less than $1 billion. And it spreads the sacrifice broadly and fairly: $24 billion in entitlement cuts, $13 billion in other spending cuts and $17 billion in new tax revenues.

The federal government must stop sending benefits to people who don't really need them. The nonpartisan Concord Coalition has a fair method that doesn't touch the majority of Americans. Taxpayers would add their income, plus the value of their entitlements, such as Social Security, Medicare, certain veterans' compensation and farm payments. If that sum was more than $40,000, their benefits would be reduced based on how far above the $40,000 line the person fell.

The reduction in benefits would be 10 percent in the $40,000–$50,000 range, and 70 percent at $100,000–$110,000. This wouldn't happen overnight, but would be phased in over five years. For Medicare beneficiaries, the means-test would be applied only to the "insurance value"—the value of a person's coverage beyond what he or she pays in premiums—and has nothing to do with how much medical care someone receives.

Saves $10 billion.

The Clinton plan lets the Medicare and Medicaid budgets rise by nearly $28 billion next year. A task force headed by Senator Judd Gregg (R.-N.H.) has recommended slowing the annual increase in Medicare to 7.5 percent by accelerating the use of HMOs, and Medicaid to 4 percent by giving states more flexibility in this federal-state program. While the 4 percent goal may be unrealistic, it is clear that well-run HMOs and other forms of "managed care" can deliver quality care and major savings.

This is the principal alternative to making beneficiaries pay more for their coverage—now that Congress has rejected the responsible course of *comprehensive* health-care reform. By accelerating managed care, the feds ought to reduce the annual increase in Medicare and Medicaid by at least 2 percent.

Saves $5 billion.

The government's cost-of-living formula over-adjusts entitlements, tax brackets and exemptions for inflation, according to experts. It should be made more accurate, using the Congressional Budget Office's conservative estimate that it's about 0.5 percent too high.

Saves $3 billion.

With people living much longer, raise the age for full benefits under Social Security—currently 65—by 3 months every year.

Saves $2 billion.

Federal pensions are generous. Yet last week, a House panel balked at making federal employees pay more toward their retirement benefits. Reasonable, yet politically sensitive, reforms could include stopping inflation-adjustments for nondisabled retirees younger than 62 and reducing the matching money on 401(k) plans.

Saves $2 billion.

As House Majority Leader Dick Armey said when he was a powerless member of the minority, U.S. agriculture subsidies are contradictory to the free market. They should be phased out over several years.

Saves $2 billion.

The Pentagon hasn't scaled back its operations to reflect who won the cold war. The Clinton budget cuts defense substantially, but it ought to be cut by billions more. Examples: Cancel the B-2 Stealth bomber, built to penetrate an Evil Empire whose remnant now can't even knock over Chechnya. Sink the Seawolf submarine. Kill the Milstar satellite system for wartime communications. Cancel the F-22 fighter.

Saves $6 billion.

Scale back intelligence-gathering.

Saves $3 billion.

The space station is super-duper, but not worth the red ink.

Saves $2 billion.

Most small-business successes have nothing to do with the Small Business Administration. Cancel most of its functions—shift anything worthwhile to Commerce.

Saves $1 billion.

Start charging market prices for hydropower sold by the Department of Energy.

Saves $1 billion.

Ross Perot was right! Raising the gas tax 50 cents a gallon would slash the deficit while discouraging gas-guzzling. Start with a dime next year.

Raises $10 billion.

Maybe the saying should be: Nothing is certain except death *or* taxes. When an investor dies, his estate escapes the tax on capital gains. Close this loophole.

Raises $3 billion.

Increase the 24-cents-a-pack cigarette tax by $1 over the next four years. This would discourage teens from taking up this expensive, unhealthy habit.

Raises $3 billion.

End the right of oil, gas and some mineral firms to deduct a percentage of their gross income.

Raises $1 billion.

This is strong medicine. It is based on a premise that real deficit reduction will happen only if elected officials have the guts to tackle substantive areas of federal spending—not the relatively small pieces some are targeting now.

It is based on a premise that Americans will forgo tax cuts, close loopholes and absorb some higher taxes in service of fiscal responsibility.

It will mean pink slips for some bureaucrats, defense workers and others. It will require a spirit of shared sacrifice from those who have benefited most from the government's growing entitlements.

But the choice is simple: The harm of chronic deficits far outweighs the hurt from making government live within its means.

QUESTIONS FOR ANALYSIS

1. Do you agree with Mr. Kasich that, "No economy, no matter how prosperous, can afford to pile up literally trillions upon trillions of dollars of debt"? Why or why not?

2. Peter Peterson argues that to increase productivity, we must invest much more, which means we must save more. Why?

3. To save more, Peterson says that we should reduce and eventually eliminate the federal deficit. Why?

4. To reduce the deficit, Peterson contends that entitlements like Social Security and Medicare must be cut. In his view, the problem is that *"[a]ll of us* have decided that we are *entitled* to much more than our society can afford to pay for. . . ."* Do you agree? Why or why not?

5. Is it really necessary that the United States reduce its budget deficit? Why or why not?

6. Are spending cuts the only way to reduce the deficit? If not, what other ways are there?

7. What cuts in government spending proposed by the *Philadelphia Inquirer* do you agree with? Which cuts do you disagree with? Why?

PART NINE

TAXATION

AND

PERSONAL

INVESTING

There is considerable interest in tax reform in the United States. The first two articles are a debate between Robert Hall and Alvin Rabushka of Stanford University, who favor a flat tax, and Robert Kuttner of the *American Prospect*, who opposes it. For investors, a related question is: what types of investments are likely to yield high returns? In the final article, Burton Malkiel of Princeton University argues that bonds are likely to be a good investment.

The Flat Tax: Alternative Views

Alvin Rabushka   Robert E. Hall

ROBERT E. HALL AND ALVIN RABUSHKA

Simplify, Simplify*

Asurge of interest in complete reform of the Federal tax system is sweeping the country and energizing Washington. One source of the desire for change is disgust with the hideously complex tax system we now have. Another is the higher economic growth that a consumption tax would bring. And a third is the anger that honest taxpayers feel about widespread tax avoidance and tax evasion in the current system.

But the public also wants to retain one important feature of the existing system: progressivity, the principle that people with higher incomes should pay a higher percentage of that income in taxes. In particular, the poor should be exempt from tax up to a reasonable level of sustenance. The nation is ready for a simple, easily enforced, progressive tax on consumption.

For more than a decade, we have been advocating a tax reform with all of these features. Both the structure of the tax and estimates of its revenue have withstood close examination by experts, including the Treasury. The tax would reproduce the revenue of the current personal and corporate taxes with just a 19 percent rate. Our idea has generally been called the flat tax. But there is much more to it than just a simpler tax schedule.

One of the most important principles is to tax business income where it is generated—in businesses—rather than after it makes its way to individual

*This article appeared in the *New York Times* on February 8, 1995. Robert Hall and Alvin Rabushka are senior fellows at the Hoover Institution at Stanford.

taxpayers in the form of interest and dividends. Right now the system allows businesses to deduct such items, then tries to collect taxes from the recipients—an inefficient procedure that invites fraud.

To tax income at its source, we propose a comprehensive business tax. It would replace the current corporate income tax, personal taxes on noncorporate businesses and personal taxation of interest and dividends. Think of it as a withholding tax on interest, dividends and other types of income people earn from business. At the individual level, we'd tax only wages, salaries and pensions.

Here is where the system is progressive—a family of four pays tax only on earnings above an exemption level of $25,500. A family earning $25,000 pays no individual tax; one earning $50,000 pays $4,655, and one earning $100,000 pays $14,155. Dividends and interest have already been taxed at the business level and are not taxed again.

And the gains in simplicity are immense. Businesses and families can file their returns on forms the size of postcards. The numbers entered on these forms are clear and easy to calculate. Opportunities for evasion are minimized. The resources needed to comply with this streamlined tax system are a tiny fraction of those consumed today by Federal income taxes.

A family would pay a 19 percent tax on the amount that its wages, salaries and pensions exceed the exemption level. A business would pay a 19 percent tax on its revenue, with deductions for purchases of materials from other businesses; for its wages, salaries and pensions, and for its purchases of capital goods.

These deductions are central to the design of the tax. The deduction for materials bought from other businesses guarantees that business income is taxed once and only once. The deduction for wages, salaries and pensions recognizes that families pay taxes on these earnings. And the deduction for purchases of capital goods (plant and equipment) makes the tax a consumption tax.

Why do the family and business taxes add up to a consumption tax? Consumption is total income minus investment in new capital. Any tax imposed on income minus investment is a consumption tax.

There are many economically equivalent ways to administer a consumption tax. One obvious way would be a national sales tax on consumption of goods and services. The trick would be to make the sales tax progressive; that would require something like a family rebate of the tax on purchases up to an exemption level. But rebates create enormous opportunities for fraud. Even today, the Internal Revenue Service is battling a huge stream of fraudulent applications for tax refunds. The taxes we propose would be the equivalent of a 19 percent Federal sales tax together with a fraud-free rebate based on earnings.

Another way to set up a consumption tax is a value-added tax—the equivalent of a sales tax, collected along the way from businesses at every stage of production instead of the point where goods are sold to consumers. The entire tax is collected from businesses; individuals don't file tax returns. Value-added taxes are universal in Europe and have proved that broad taxes on consumption are feasible. But like a sales tax, a VAT is not progressive: it taxes a family's consumption from the first dollar. The only way to make it progressive is to issue rebates, and this opens the door for fraud.

The last way to set up a tax on consumption is to impose a tax on individuals, measuring consumption as what they earn minus what they save. Like our plan, the individual consumption tax is progressive without a rebate because it has a tax form for individuals and taxes are limited to the amount of consumption over an exemption level.

But an individual consumption tax would be an administrative nightmare. Not only would individuals have to report all types of income (rather than relying on universal withholding), but the IRS would have to keep track of billions of new items to measure saving. Dishonest taxpayers would overstate their payments into savings accounts and understate their withdrawals. True simplification and efficiency cannot be achieved with a family consumption tax.

Consider the goals we started with. Tax only consumption. Tax it progressively. Make it easy to comply and hard to commit fraud. The system embodied in our two post-card-sized forms is the unique proposal that delivers them all.

The Flat Tax: Alternative Views

ROBERT KUTTNER

Instead, Close Loopholes*

Tax all business and personal income at a flat rate, say 17 or 19 percent. Eliminate all deductions, depreciation schedules and other complications. Raise the personal exemption, so moderate-income households pay little or no tax. It sounds wonderful.

But on closer examination, the logic of such "flat tax" plans falls apart. Behind the promise of simplicity and tax reduction are higher deficits and a more regressive tax system.

The leading proposal on the table right now is by Representative Richard Armey of Texas, the House majority leader. As drafted, it would cost the Treasury more than $200 billion a year. To be truly revenue-neutral, it would require a rate of more than 25 percent, increasing taxes on all but the wealthiest payers.

The silliest part of the "flat tax" notion is the very premise that simplification requires a single rate. Tax rates, of course, are not what makes taxation complex. For individuals and businesses, calculating the rate is the easy part. Whether the schedule is flat or graduated, you just multiply taxable income by the applicable rate. The complicated part is figuring out what constitutes taxable income—what should be deducted, if anything, before you calculate your taxes.

*This article also appeared in the *New York Times* on February 8, 1995. Robert Kuttner is co-editor of the *American Prospect*.

Eliminating deductions would obviously simplify the tax system. But some tax preferences, like the mortgage interest deduction, serve good social purposes, and others, like the deduction for medical expenses, reflect the fact that if you earn $60,000 and have to spend $30,000 on doctor and hospital bills, you don't have the same resources as a healthy person who makes $60,000. Mr. Armey would do away with both.

Businesses' taxable income, likewise, is no simple matter to calculate. If we swept away the complex treatment of business income and expenses, a lot of businesses would be taxed on their expenses as well as their profits.

The more serious mischief in the flat tax campaign is the tired claim that we can have a free lunch: lower taxes for most people and no effect on the budget. Mr. Armey says this is possible since "as the economy grows because of the favorable treatment of savings, investment and low marginal tax rates, revenue to the Treasury will grow."

If this sounds familiar, it's because under its old name—supply-side economics—it was discredited by a full field test in the 1980s. Ronald Reagan's supply-side tax cuts never delivered their promised revenue increases; deficits became chronic and the national debt tripled. Conversely, during the long postwar boom, rates on the richest taxpayers were as high as 91 percent and the economy did just fine. And ever since the top tax rate was raised in the 1993 budget accord, the economy has been growing at least 4 percent a year.

The Treasury Department calculated last fall that far from raising more money, a flat tax of 17 percent would reduce tax receipts by $244 billion a year. Mr. Armey complained that the Treasury had misunderstood certain technical aspects of the bill, such as the interaction of income and payroll taxes. Treasury disagreed, but found that even accepting Mr. Armey's technical adjustments, the plan would still lose $186 billion a year.

An analysis by Citizens for Tax Justice, based on the Treasury findings, calculates that a revenue-neutral version of the Armey plan would require a flat rate of 25.8 percent. That would mean higher taxes for every income group—except people making $200,000 or more. That group would enjoy an average tax cut of $28,410.

Mr. Armey's plan, like other such proposals, was inspired by the economists Robert Hall and Alvin Rabushka, whose 1983 book *Low Tax, Simple Tax* promised similar miracles (with similar mathematical ingenuity). But even Mr. Hall has been quoted as estimating that the Armey plan would require a 23 percent tax rate to break even; and the Hall-Rabushka book acknowledged that a flat tax would be "a tremendous boon to the economic elite" and that "lower taxes on the successful will have to be made up by higher taxes on average people."

The tax system can be greatly simplified without giving up graduated rates. The 1986 Tax Reform Act, sponsored by Representative Richard Gephardt of Missouri and Senator Bill Bradley of New Jersey, cut rates top and bottom, and paid for the cuts by closing loopholes. President Clinton's 1993 tax amendments paid for tax relief at the bottom by raising rates at the top.

There are still plenty of loopholes that don't make economic sense. Large inheritances are so shielded from taxes that the estate tax is mostly, as a Brookings Institution study dryly termed it, "voluntary." Tax breaks for second homes and lavish deductions of business expenses can be eliminated to cut taxes on working families.

Nobody likes taxes. But if we are to have public services at all, it makes sense to pay for them by taxing wealthy people at higher rates than the middle and working class. Mr. Gephardt, now the House minority leader, recently proposed that by closing additional loopholes, we could reduce rates and yet retain a system at least as progressive as the current one. The Gephardt approach has been described in some quarters as a Democratic flat tax, yet another case of Democrats embracing Republican ideas. It is not. It is a marriage of tax simplification and tax fairness—without raiding the Treasury.

The very idea of a flat tax is a reversal of the well-established principle of taxation based on ability to pay. Progressive taxation dates to Woodrow Wilson. It is sensible economics, popular politics and sound fiscal policy. Democrats would make a big mistake to borrow the "flat tax" concept—or the label.

Bonds Are Good Investments*

BURTON MALKIEL

L et's now turn to an assessment of the bond market. High-quality corporate bond yields, while well below the early 1980s peak, were in mid-1995 around 8 percent and still reasonably generous. Remember that inflation rates have also come down sharply. While it is true that the measured rate of inflation in the United States rose to about 5 percent at the end of the 1980s, recent wage behavior and productivity trends suggest a core inflation rate at the start of 1995 of no more than 3 to 4 percent. This gives a projected very generous real rate of return of something in the vicinity of 4 to 5 percent, not too much lower in real terms than earlier in the eighties. Thus, bonds in mid-1995 were priced to be a very serviceable investment that should provide unusually generous real rates of return. Over the long pull in the United States, corporate bonds have historically produced a real rate of return of only 2 percent, as measured by Ibbotson and Sinquefield.

Comparisons of prospective stock and bond yields can potentially be very helpful to investors. The following figure plots bond yields and prospective rates of return on common stocks (the Dow Jones industrial average), calculated using the growth-rate estimates of Wall Street analysts. The figure shows that bond yields rose above the prospective returns from stocks only

*Burton Malkiel is professor of economics at Princeton University. This is an excerpt from his *A Random Walk down Wall Street,* 6th ed. (New York: Norton, 1996).

CHART 1   Expected Total Return: Stocks and Bonds

once. That was during the early autumn of 1987. When even U.S. government bonds rose above 10 percent, this proved far too competitive for common stocks and the market collapsed. While I would never claim that any statistic can reliably predict turns in the market, such comparisons can at least be helpful in providing warning signals and revealing periods of attractive relative values in the bond market. As of mid-1995, bonds appeared to offer return possibilities almost as attractive as stocks but with less risk.

Bonds are the Rodney Dangerfield of financial investments. They don't get much respect. The arguments against bonds are easy to make. Over the long pull, their total return (interest payments plus capital gains and losses) has been far inferior to that of common stocks. Over the past sixty years, stocks have returned a compound annual rate of 10 percent, about 7 percentage points better than the average rate of inflation over the period. On the other hand, high-grade corporate bonds have eked out a rate of return of only about 5 percent. In inflation-adjusted terms, bonds yielded 2 percent versus 7 percent for stocks; thus, stocks did 3½ times as well as bonds.

With the benefit of hindsight, we now know that bonds were inappropriately priced thirty years ago (as they also were in the forties and early fifties when their yields were pegged at artificially low levels). If investors had known thirty years ago that inflation would become a major problem—if they had correctly forecast that the general economy, inflation rates, exchange rates, and, therefore, interest rates would become increasingly volatile—bonds would not have been priced to give such inadequate total returns. But remember that our smartest economists were claiming in the early 1960s that inflation (then at 1 percent) was dead and that even minor fluctuations in economic activity could easily be offset. Economists and investors were egregiously wrong. But they are not likely to be wrong forever.

The point is that you shouldn't invest with a rearview mirror. What was a poor investment over the past sixty years will not necessarily be one over the next sixty. Investors learn, and new information about inflation and volatility does get incorporated into market prices. Bonds today reflect the poorer inflation outlook and the greater instability of bond prices. The issue is not how poorly bond investors fared in the 1950s, 1960s, and 1970s. The issue is: Will bonds produce a generous return in the future? I believe that when purchased at the 8 percent yield levels existing as of mid-1995, the answer is yes. . . .

COULD I BE WRONG?

The thesis presented is that at the price levels existing in mid-1995, attractive prospective returns are likely to come in the future from investment in bonds. Stocks appear to be, at best, of average attractiveness. A popular maxim warns, however, "If you can remain calm when everyone around you is panicked, perhaps you don't understand the problem." Could the problem be worse than I have described? Could the market actually be underestimating the long-run inflation dangers to economic instability? What if the core rate of inflation is about to ratchet back up to the double-digit level, as some investors fear? This is precisely the situation that would make my investment thesis wrong as it concerns long-term bonds. (And it would undoubtedly make investment in tangible assets far more attractive than was the case in the 1980s.) So the critical final question I must address is the likelihood that the current core inflation rate will remain at a restrained level.

While many forecasters anticipate a sharp acceleration of inflation in the late 1990s, I would suggest to you that there are at least some reasons for optimism as well as some for concern. The most favorable part of the picture concerns the behavior of wage settlements. Average hourly earnings are still rising at less than a 4 percent rate. I realize that many analysts believe that the recent period of wage restraint is an aberration and that a significant acceleration of wage settlements is likely. But even if this were true, the tightening of controls throughout American industry and the increasing experience mix of our labor force augur well for a better productivity performance in the late 1990s. Thus, the rise in unit labor costs (which I have suggested is a good proxy for the core rate of inflation) should not increase by more than 4 percent and may do even better.

Over the longer term, however, there are also reasons to be sanguine. I think we have learned throughout the Western world that our economies do not work well with high and variable rates of inflation, and there is now a willingness to accept far harsher demand management policies than was previously thought politically feasible. The level of unemployment throughout the Western world was higher in the mid-1990s, and was expected to stay higher than at similar points of postwar economic cycles. Moreover, even socialist European Economic Community countries were experiencing unprecedented high rates of unemployment. While there should be considerable growth in the less-developed world and in formerly communist countries, it seems quite likely that the world economy will not be characterized by excess demand and increases in the prices of basic commodities. Our past problem with inflation was associated with world-wide excess demand or at least tight supply conditions.

Moreover, U.S. labor clearly recognizes that our economy is now sufficiently open to world trade that continued reasonable moderation in industrial wage demands and acceptance of changes in work rules are essential if we are to keep from becoming a service economy. An industry-by-industry analysis suggests that heightened competitive pressures in both domestic and foreign markets (and including substantially increased competition from developing countries) have significantly changed the wage-setting process. Moreover, the deregulation of such industries as airlines, trucking, and telephone service has triggered increased wage competition in many industries. While no one can tell if we will succeed, there are certainly reasons for optimism that the upward ratcheting of the core inflation rate has ended.

There is, however, one disturbing part of the picture that has not yet fallen into place in the United States and is, I believe, the reason interest rates are still as high as they are and threaten to return to even higher levels. The projected federal budget deficit in the mid-1990s is still far too large. More disturbing is the fact that most projections show the deficit rising in the late 1990s with the aging of the U.S. population. It is clear that political action with respect to the budget will be necessary to remove the legitimate fear that interest rates will increase as private and federal demands overwhelm the supply of savings or that continued deficit spending will eventually lead to inflation. Progress on the deficit would remove an important question mark on the thesis presented, at least as it concerns investment in bonds. Even if less progress is made than desirable, I believe that bonds will provide reasonable real rates of return over the remainder of the 1990s. At the very least, investors should assign some substantial probability to this continued moderate inflation scenario (or at least no return to the 1970s inflation scenario) and balance their equity positions with some portion of their investment funds in bonds.

It is also well to remember . . . that capital markets are at least reasonably efficient over the long pull. Fears about renewed inflation and economic instability are not reflected in stock and bond prices at some time in the future; they are reflected in the market now. If investors perceive that investment risk has increased, the financial pages reflect such thinking very quickly. In well-functioning financial markets, such as ours, investors are willing to buy only those assets that will provide the higher future rates of return sufficient to compensate them for added risk.

Does my expectation for reasonably attractive rates of return from bonds and stocks mean that I am predicting a bull market rally during some specific period of the late 1990s? Not at all! As a random walker through Wall Street, I am skeptical that anyone can predict the course of short-term stock price movements, and perhaps we are better off for it. I am reminded of one of my favorite episodes from the marvelous old radio serial "I Love a Mystery." This mystery was about a greedy stock-market investor who wished that just once he would be allowed to see the paper, with its stock price changes, twenty-four hours in advance. By some occult twist his wish was granted, and early in the evening he received the late edition of the next day's paper. He worked feverishly through the night planning early-morning purchases and late-afternoon sales which would guarantee him a killing in the market. Then, before his elation had diminished, he read through the remainder of the paper—and came upon his own obituary. His servant found him dead the next morning.

Since I, fortunately, do not have access to future newspapers, I cannot tell how stock and bond prices will behave in any particular period ahead. Nevertheless, I am convinced that the long-run estimates of bond and stock returns presented here are the most reasonable ones that can be made for investment planning during the remainder of the 1990s and into the twenty-first century. Investors will, I believe, be well served by putting their money where my mouth is and investing a substantial part of their wealth in paper assets, including bonds.

QUESTIONS FOR ANALYSIS

1. Professors Hall and Rabushka argue for a tax on consumption expenditure, not on income. What are the advantages of such a tax?

2. Mr. Kuttner argues strongly for progressive taxation—that is, for the principle that tax rates should be higher for the affluent than for the poor. Do Professors Hall and Rabushka reject this argument?

3. According to Professors Hall and Rabushka, their form of a flat tax is preferable to a value-added tax. Why?

4. Why are bonds the "Rodney Dangerfield" of investment?

5. Explain why Professor Malkiel believes that bonds are a good investment.

PART TEN

MONETARY

POLICY

In the mid-1990s, there was considerable and continuous controversy over monetary policy. Many observers believed that the Federal Reserve's policies were not sufficiently expansionary; others felt that the opposite was true. The first article in this part is the testimony of Alan Greenspan, chairman of the Fed, before the House Banking Committee in 1993. The second article is an attack on the policies announced in Greenspan's testimony by Henry Gonzalez, chairman of the House Banking Committee. The third article, by Alan Blinder, discusses what the Federal Reserve's objectives should be.

The Fed Aims for Price Stability*

ALAN GREENSPAN

Thank you for this opportunity to discuss the Federal Reserve's semi-annual monetary policy report to the Congress. My remarks this morning will cover the current monetary policy and economic settings, as well as the Federal Reserve's longer-term strategy for contributing, to the best of our abilities, to the nation's economic well-being.

As the economic expansion has progressed somewhat fitfully, our earlier characterization of the economy as facing stiff headwinds has appeared increasingly appropriate. Doubtless the major headwind in this regard has been the combined efforts of households, businesses, and financial institutions to repair and to rebuild their balance sheets following the damage inflicted in recent years as weakening asset values exposed excessive debt burdens.

But there have been other headwinds as well. The build-down of national defense has cast a shadow over particular industries and regions of the country. Spending on nonresidential real estate dropped dramatically in the face of overbuilding and high vacancy rates, and has remained in the doldrums. At the same time, corporations across a wide range of industries have been making efforts to pare employment and expenses in order to im-

*This testimony was presented before the Committee on Banking, Finance, and Urban Affairs of the U.S. House of Representatives on July 20, 1993. Alan Greenspan is chairman of the Board of Governors of the Federal Reserve System.

prove productivity and their competitive positions. These efforts have been prompted in part by innovative technologies, which have been applied to almost every area of economic endeavor, and have boosted investment. However, their effect on jobs and wages through much of the expansion also has made households more cautious spenders.

In the past several years, as these influences have restrained the economy, they have been balanced in part by the accommodative stance of monetary policy and, more recently, by declines in longer-term interest rates as the prospects for credible federal deficit cuts improved. From the time monetary policy began to move toward ease in 1989 to now, short-term interest rates have dropped by more than two-thirds and long-term rates have declined substantially too. All along the maturity spectrum, interest rates have come down to their lowest levels in twenty or thirty years, aiding the repair of balance sheets, bolstering the cash flow of borrowers, and providing support for interest-sensitive spending.

The process of easing monetary policy, however, had to be closely controlled and generally gradual, because of the constraint imposed by the marketplace's acute sensitivity to inflation. As I pointed out in my February testimony to the Congress, this is a constraint that did not exist in an earlier time. Before the late 1970s, financial market participants and others apparently believed that, while inflationary pressures might surface from time to time, the institutional structure of the U.S. economy simply would not permit sustained inflation. But as inflation and, consequently, long-term interest rates soared into the double digits at the end of the 1970s, investors became painfully aware that they had underestimated the economy's potential for inflation. As a result, monetary policy in recent years has had to remain alert to the possibility that an ill-timed easing could be undone by a flare-up of inflation expectations, pushing long-term interest rates higher, and short-circuiting essential balance sheet repair.

The cumulative monetary easing over the last four years has been very substantial. Since last September, however, no further steps have been taken, as the stance of policy has appeared broadly appropriate to the evolving economic circumstances.

That stance has been quite accommodative, especially judging by the level of real short-term interest rates in the context of, on average, moderate economic growth. Short-term real interest rates have been in the neighborhood of zero over the last three quarters. In maintaining this accommodative stance, we have been persuaded by the evidence of persistent slack in labor and product markets, increasing international competitiveness, and the decided absence of excessive credit and money expansion. The forces that engendered past inflationary episodes appear to have been lacking to date.

DISTURBING INDICATIONS OF INFLATION

Yet some of the readings on inflation earlier this year were disturbing. It appeared that prices might be accelerating despite product market slack and an unemployment rate noticeably above estimates of the so-called "natural" rate of unemployment—that is, the rate at which price pressures remain roughly constant. In the past, the existing degree of slack in the economy had been consistent with continuing disinflation.

However, the inflation outcome, history tells us, depends not only on the amount of slack remaining in labor and product markets, but on other factors as well, including the rate at which that slack is changing. If the economy is growing rapidly, inflation pressures can arise, even in the face of excess capacity, as temporary bottlenecks emerge and as workers and producers raise wages and prices in anticipation of continued strengthening in demand. Near the end of last year, about the time many firms probably were finalizing their plans for 1993, sales and capacity utilization were moving up markedly and there was a surge of optimism about future economic activity. This may well have set in motion a wave of price increases, which showed through to broad measures of prices earlier this year.

Moreover, inflation expectations, at least by some measures, appear to have tilted upward this year, possibly contributing to price pressures. The University of Michigan survey of consumer attitudes, for example, reported an increase in the inflation rate expected to prevail over the next 12 months from about 3.75 percent in the fourth quarter of last year to nearly 4.5 percent in the second quarter of this year. Preliminary data imply some easing of such expectations earlier this month, but the sample from which those data are derived is too small to be persuasive. Moreover, the price of gold, which can be broadly reflective of inflationary expectations, has risen sharply in recent months. And at times this spring, bond yields spiked higher when incoming news about inflation was most discouraging.

The role of expectations in the inflation process is crucial. Even expectations not validated by economic fundamentals can themselves add appreciably to wage and price pressures for a considerable period, potentially derailing the economy from its growth track.

Why, for example, despite an above-normal rate of unemployment and permanent layoffs, have uncertainties about job security not led to further moderation in wage increases? The answer appears to lie, at least in part, in the deep-seated anticipations understandably harbored by workers that inflation is likely to reaccelerate in the near term and undercut their real wages.

The Federal Open Market Committee (FOMC) became concerned that inflation expectations and price pressures, unless contained, could raise long-term interest rates and stall economic expansion. Consequently, at its meeting in May, while affirming the more accommodative policy stance in place since last September, the FOMC also deemed it appropriate to initiate a so-called asymmetric directive. Such a directive, with its bias in the direction of a possible firming of policy over the inter-meeting period, does not prejudge that action will be taken—and indeed none occurred. But it did indicate that further signs of a potential deterioration of the inflation outlook would merit serious consideration of whether short-term rates needed to be raised slightly from their relatively low levels to ensure that financial conditions remained conducive to sustained growth.

Certainly the May and June price figures have helped assuage concerns that new inflationary pressures had taken hold. Nonetheless, on balance, the news on inflation this year must be characterized as disappointing. Despite disinflationary forces and continued slack, the rate of inflation has, at best, stabilized, rather than easing further as past relationships would have suggested.

In assessing the stance of monetary policy and the likelihood of persistent inflationary pressures, the FOMC took account of the downshift in the pace of economic expansion earlier this year. This downshift left considerable remaining slack in the economy and promised that the adverse price movements prompted by the acceleration in growth late last year likely would deminish. . .

Over the last two years, the forces of restraint on the economy have changed, but real growth has continued, with one sector of the economy after another taking the lead. Against this background, Federal Reserve Board governors and Reserve Bank presidents project that the U.S. economy will remain on the moderate growth path it has been following as the expansion has progressed. Their forecasts for real GDP average around 2.5 percent from the fourth quarter of 1992 to the fourth quarter of 1993, and cluster around 2.5 to 3.25 percent over the four quarters of 1994. Reflecting this moderate rise and the outlook for labor productivity, unemployment is generally expected to edge lower, to around 6.75 percent by the end of this year, and to perhaps a shade lower by the end of next year. For this year as a whole, FOMC participants see inflation at or just above 3 percent, and most of them have the same forecast for next year.

In addition to focusing on the outlook for the economy at its July meeting, the FOMC, as required by the Humphrey-Hawkins Act, set ranges for the growth of money and debt for this year, and, on a preliminary basis, for 1994. One premise of the discussion of the ranges was that the uncharacteristically slow growth of the broad monetary aggregates in the last couple of years—and the atypical increases in their velocities—would persist for a while longer. M2 has been far weaker than income and interest rates would predict. Indeed, if the historical relationships between M2 and nominal income had remained intact, the behavior of M2 in recent years would have been consistent with an economy in severe contraction. To an important degree, the behavior of M2 has reflected structural changes in the financial sector: The thrift industry has downsized by necessity, and commercial banks have pulled back as well, largely reflecting the burgeoning loan losses that followed the lax lending of earlier years. With depository credit weak, there has been little bidding for deposits, and depositors, in any case, have been drawn to the higher returns on capital market instruments. Inflows to bond and stock mutual funds have reached record levels, and, to the extent that these inflows have come at the expense of growth in deposits or money-market mutual funds, the broad monetary aggregates have been depressed.

In this context, the FOMC lowered the 1993 ranges for M2 and M3 to 1-to-5 percent and 0-to-4 percent, respectively. This represents a reduction of one percentage point in the M2 range and a half percentage point for M3. Even with these reductions, we would not be surprised to see the monetary aggregates finish the year near the lower ends of their ranges.

MONETARY AGGREGATE ESTIMATES NO LONGER RELIABLE

As I emphasized in a similar context in February, the lowering of the ranges is purely a technical matter; it does not indicate, nor should it be perceived as, a shift of monetary policy in the direction of restraint. It is indicative merely of the state of our knowledge about the factors depressing the growth of the aggregates relative to spending, of the course of the aggregates to date, and of the likelihood of various outcomes through the end of the year. While the lowering of the range reflects our judgment that shifts out of M2 will persist, the upper end of the revised range allows for a resumption of more normal behavior, or even some unwinding of M2 shortfalls. The FOMC also lowered the 1993 range for debt of the domestic nonfinancial sectors, by a half percentage point, to 4-to-8 percent. The debt aggregate is likely to come in comfortably within its new range, as it continues growing about in line with nominal GDP. The new ranges for growth of money and debt in 1993 were carried over on a preliminary basis into 1994.

In reading the longer-run intentions of the FOMC, the specific ranges need to be interpreted cautiously. The historical relationships between money and income, and between money and the price level, have largely broken down, depriving the aggregates of much of their usefulness as guides to policy. At least for the time being, M2 has been downgraded as a reliable indicator of financial conditions in the economy, and no single variable has yet been identified to take its place. . .

In these circumstances, it is especially prudent to focus on longer-term policy guides. One important guidepost is real interest rates, which have a key bearing on longer-run spending decisions and inflation prospects.

In assessing real rates, the central issue is their relationship to an equilibrium interest rate, specifically the real rate level that, if maintained, would keep the economy at its production potential over time. Rates persisting above that level, history tells us, tend to be associated with slack, disinflation, and economic stagnation—below that level with eventual resource bottlenecks and rising inflation, which ultimately engenders economic contraction. Maintaining the real rate around its equilibrium level should have a stabilizing effect on the economy, directing production toward its long-term potential.

The level of the equilibrium real rate—or, more appropriately, the equilibrium term structure of real rates—cannot be estimated with a great deal of confidence, though with enough to be useful for monetary policy. Real rates, of course, are not directly observable, but must be inferred from nominal interest rates and estimates of inflation expectations. The most important real rates for private spending decisions almost surely are the longer maturities. Moreover, the equilibrium rate structure responds to the ebb and flow of underlying forces affecting spending. So, for example, in recent years, the appropriate real rate structure doubtless has been depressed by the headwinds of balance sheet restructuring and fiscal retrenchment. Despite the uncertainties about the levels of equilibrium and actual real interest rates, rough judgments about these variables can be made and used in conjunction with other indicators in the monetary policy process. Currently, short-term real rates, most directly affected by the Federal Reserve, are not far from zero; long-term rates, set primarily by the market, are appreciably higher, judging from the steep slope of the yield curve and reasonable suppositions about inflation expectations. This configuration indicates that market participants anticipate that short-term real rates will have to rise as the headwinds diminish, if substantial inflationary imbalances are to be avoided. . .

I believe we are on our way toward reestablishing the trust in the purchasing power of the dollar that is crucial to maximizing and fulfilling the productivity capacity of this nation. The public, however, clearly remains to be convinced: Survey responses and financial market prices embody expectations that the current lower level of inflation not only will not be bettered, it will not even persist. But there are glimmers of hope that trust is reemerging. For example, issuers have found receptive markets in recent months for fifty-year bonds. This had not happened in decades. The reopening of that market may be read as one indication that some investors once again believe that inflationary pressures will remain subdued.

It is my firm belief that, with fiscal consolidation and with the monetary policy path that we have charted, the United States is well-positioned to remain at the forefront of the world economy well into the next century.

An Open Letter to the President*

HENRY B. GONZALEZ

Dear President Clinton:

I am very disappointed with Federal Reserve Chairman Alan Greenspan's announcement Tuesday [July 20] that the Federal Reserve will ratchet down the targets for money growth from 2 to 6 percent to 1 to 5 percent. The Federal Reserve has failed to meet its own targets for a year and a half, and now is moving the targets down to actual recession levels of money growth. With new reports that the industrial sector actually shrunk in June and consumer confidence fell, a policy that allows one percent growth in our nation's money supply will cause continued hardship for our nation's workers and families.

The Federal Reserve decision-makers have lowered their range for the projected real Gross Domestic Product (GDP) growth in 1993 from their February 1993 estimate of 2.5 to 4.0 percent, to their new estimate of 2.0 to 3.5 percent. Slow growth of 2.0 to 2.5 percent is within their projected plans.

Instead of this continued policy of virtually no growth, this is the time to urge the Federal Reserve to follow a monetary policy that is consistent with your policies to put our citizens back to work. The money supply (defined as M2) should be growing at least as fast as the production of goods

*This letter was written on July 22, 1993. Henry B. Gonzalez was chairman of the Committee on Banking, Finance, and Urban Affairs of the U.S. House of Representatives.

and services in a full employment economy. A growth rate of 4.5 percent for M2 falls in the middle of the Federal Reserve's money supply target range for 1992 and would be appropriate. With the economy stagnating as it is, a small increase in the money supply is not enough to reignite inflation.

I urge you to consider changing the composition of the Federal Open Market Committee (FOMC) which decides our nation's monetary policies. The current Federal Reserve decision-makers are seven Reagan-Bush appointees at the Board of Governors. The twelve Federal Reserve presidents are selected by their Bank board of directors, who mostly represent commercial banks.

In general, the Federal Reserve decision-makers are bankers or friends of bankers. Decision-makers representing the concerns of agriculture, small business, labor, consumer, and community groups are almost unheard of. Yet advocates of price stability even at the price of stagnation are well-represented at the FOMC.

It is long past time to change the Federal Reserve's inbred network by appointing people who are competent in central bank policy, including monetary policy. There are many competent women and minorities who never get a chance to serve on the FOMC because they cannot rise up through the old boy's bank network. Competency—not who you know in the banking world, and the ability to think for yourself and not just to march in lockstep—should top the list of requirements for being selected to the FOMC. I know that you have sought diversity and competence when making appointments in your administration, and I applaud you for that.

When Governor Wayne D. Angell's term expires on January 31, 1994, you will have the opportunity to put a different face on the Federal Reserve. Your nominee could achieve considerable clout. Not only will he or she serve as a Federal Reserve Governor, the nominee could also become the board's vice-chairman when David W. Mullins, Jr.'s term as vice-chairman ends July 24, 1995. Although Governor Mullins's term as governor does not end until January 31, 1996, you will have to select the vice-chairman in 1995 from among the sitting governors.

Last week, the Fed selected one of their own, William J. McDonough, as president of the New York Federal Reserve Bank. Mr. McDonough's qualifications and his views on monetary policy, on zero inflation, on regulation of the banking industry, and on consumer issues, will not be debated in public. His expertise in central bank monetary policy will not be questioned in Senate confirmation hearings. However, because he has been selected through the Federal Reserve's internal private mechanisms, he will manage our nation's money supply without ever going before the American people or their representatives.

I urge you to consider changing the law so that the twelve Federal Reserve Bank presidents would be appointed by the President and approved by the Senate, as is currently the case with candidates for Federal Reserve Governor. Because monetary policy is so crucial to the economy's well-being, it is essential that the public have some say over who will be controlling the money supply which affects inflation, employment, interest rates, and the international value of our currency. Meanwhile, I again respectfully urge you to encourage the Federal Reserve to follow policies more consistent with a reasonable level of growth. This can be done without reigniting inflation, whereas current policies are certain to lead to continued stagnation, decline, and hardships for millions who look to you for hope, and for change.

Sincerely,

Henry B. Gonzalez, Chairman

Reflections of a Central Banker*

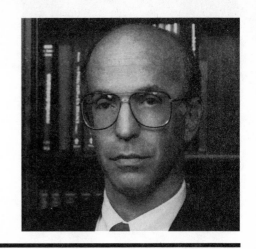

ALAN BLINDER

Iam here today in a very new role for me. While I am not young by any
reasonable criterion, I am very young as a central banker. I've been
here at the Kansas City Fed conferences in Jackson Hole several times
before, but always as an academic speaker, where my role was clearly to say
something and maybe even to say something interesting. It is quite clear
that, in my new job, my new role is to say nothing and certainly not to say
anything interesting.

Mindful of that dictum, I'd like to take us back to the perspective of a
central banker, which is to say back to macroeconomics—a subject we
haven't talked about very much in the symposium in general, but especially
not this morning. (That is not criticism at all; I feel it was quite appropriate
to discuss the things we have discussed this morning.) In particular, I was
very glad to see, when I received the program, that this is a conference
about *reducing*, not *increasing*, unemployment. Charts 1 and 2 (eight panels
in all) illustrate what a woman from Mars who landed here in Jackson Hole
to look at the unemployment history of the world since 1970 would have
seen: the standardized (by the Organization for Economic Cooperation
and Development [OECD]) unemployment rates of a nonrandomly se-

*This is an excerpt from a paper presented at a symposium at Jackson Hole, Wyoming, on
August 27, 1994. Alan Blinder, now professor of economics at Princeton University, was then
vice-chairman of the Board of Governors of the Federal Reserve System.

CHART 1   Standardized Unemployment Rates

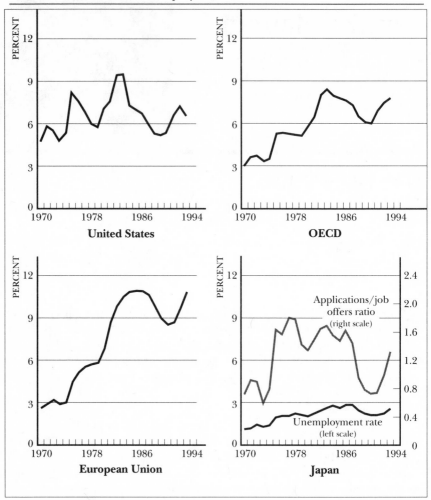

Sources: OECD Main Economic Indicators.

lected sample. The eight panels cover every country represented on the program—including the OECD and the European Union as countries—except, I'm sorry to say, New Zealand. That's because the OECD does not have a standardized unemployment rate for New Zealand that goes back this far. So this is the entire available sample. The hypothetical woman from Mars could be forgiven for wondering if the governments of these countries were really worrying about *reducing* unemployment during this

CHART 2 Standardized Unemployment Rates

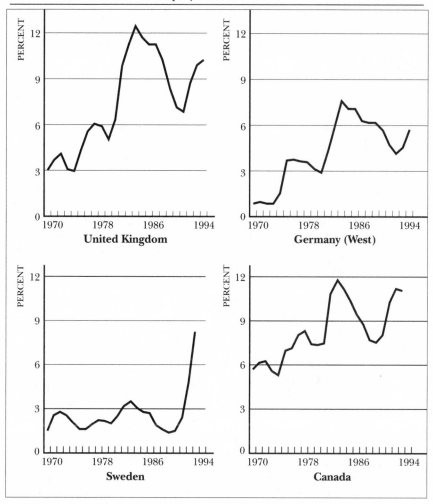

Sources: OECD Main Economic Indicators.

period rather than *increasing* unemployment. If they were worrying about reducing it, they weren't doing too well—except perhaps for Japan and the United States.

Now, in my view, central banks, or more generally macroeconomic policies, do indeed have a role in reducing unemployment as well as, not incidentally, in reducing inflation. Before I pursue that point further, there is a preliminary point—actually a hurdle which, if not jumped, leaves nothing more to say on the subject. That hurdle is this: for a central bank to have any role in either raising or reducing unemployment, you have to believe in Keynesianism. If you don't, changes in aggregate demand are all dissipated in prices right away—up or down—and you just don't have any ability to affect the unemployment rate.

The *Fortune Encyclopedia of Economics* has a definition of Keynesian economics. I wrote it, so I know what's in it. I am only going to summarize the first half of it, which is the definition of *positive* Keynesianism, forgetting about any *normative* considerations. This definition has three pieces, and I'll just read them briefly. First, it says: "A Keynesian believes that aggregate demand is influenced by a host of economic decisions—both public and private—and sometimes behaves erratically. The public decisions include, most prominently, those on monetary and fiscal (i.e., spending and tax) policy."

Second, it says that a Keynesian believes that: ". . . changes in aggregate demand, whether anticipated or unanticipated, have their greatest short-run impact on real output and employment, not on prices."

And third: "Keynesians believe that prices and, especially, wages respond slowly to changes in supply and demand, resulting in shortages and surpluses, especially of labor."

That is at least one person's definition of what it means to be Keynesian, in a positive sense. Now, by this definition, I submit that President Nixon had it right when he said, "We are all Keynesians now." (I think he said this in the 1970s.) Money is not neutral, and I don't think I have to take any time to defend that proposition any longer—although I must say that, if this were a conference of academics, I probably would. If you accept this proposition, then I can go on. If you don't, of course, I can sit down right now. (I suppose I shouldn't put that to a vote!)

If you accept this proposition and you accept the natural rate hypothesis, which has been thoroughly discussed at this meeting, they lead to what I like to call "the approximate dichotomy." I'll come at the end to why it is only "approximate"—or at least one reason why—but this is what I mean by the approximate dichotomy: where employment is concerned, in the short run macroeconomics is everything and in the long run macroeconomics is nothing.

Let me elaborate slightly on what I mean by that. In the short run, changes in aggregate demand can and do easily change the unemployment rate by, say, plus or minus two percentage points. Such events happen frequently in business cycles. There is nothing, I submit, that we know in the way of microeconomic interventions that could have an effect remotely close to that in the United States—certainly not in the short run, and maybe not even in the long run. So that's one-half of the dichotomy.

However, in the long run the meaning of the natural rate hypothesis, as Dale Mortensen stated clearly this morning, is that the unemployment rate will converge to the natural rate *regardless of macroeconomic policy*. And that means, roughly speaking, that the employment rate of five to ten years from now has nothing to do with today's macroeconomic policy. The latter is totally irrelevant. Today's macroeconomic policy will, however, have something to do with the price level of five to ten years from now.

I emphasize this dichotomy because, while it is mother's milk to economists, it is almost totally unknown outside the economics profession—indeed it is a totally foreign doctrine. Very few people have in their heads the notion that the effects of aggregate demand on jobs are temporary, which is not to say ephemeral—I don't mean they are gone in three to six months, they are certainly not—but temporary. Nor do most people realize that a very big microeconomic achievement, at least in the United States, might be reducing the natural rate of unemployment by 0.25 percent. That would be a major, major achievement. But I think that very few people outside the economics profession understand either part of this dichotomy, which is a shame.

In view of this approximate dichotomy, what is a poor central banker to do? My view is that we should remember a television quiz show that I occasionally watched in my wasted youth called *The Price Is Right*. You may remember that on *The Price Is Right* an object would appear, and contestants were supposed to guess the price. You won if you came as close to the actual price as possible *without going over*. That was the name of the game. Similarly, in my view, the job of a central bank, in this regard, is to guide the employment rate up to its natural rate, but not higher than that. By that criterion, I think the United States is extremely close to being "on target," but the European Union, I believe, is quite far from being on target.

I have stated quite clearly, I think, that I believe the central bank does have a role in reducing unemployment, or raising employment. But, as we know, not all central banks explicitly recognize an employment objective of that sort. We heard very eloquently at lunch yesterday, from Mr. Brash, the virtues of single-minded concentration on an inflation, or a price level, objective. The charge given by the Congress to the Federal Reserve is quite different, as many of you know. It calls upon us to pursue *both* maximum employment *and* stable prices. Since these two objectives conflict in the short run, the Federal Reserve Act calls upon us to strike a balance. That has always seemed very appropriate to me.

In thinking about the fact that different central banks have quite different stated objectives, I started to wonder whether the objectives actually matter. And, while I was wondering about that, I stumbled upon something which some of you have seen before: a ranking of central banks by Alex Cukierman and two coauthors. (See Chart 3.) Cukierman *et al.* rated 21 industrial countries by what they called "central bank independence." Actually, I think this was quite a big misnomer because, if you notice, the United States is ranked pretty low. And I can tell you we feel fairly independent at the Fed, at least inside the building. In fact, the rankings really rate central banks on the singlemindedness of their concentration on inflation reduction, or price-level stability. Here, again, I must apologize to New Zealand. I didn't make up these rankings, and they came before the Reserve Bank Act of 1989. New Zealand, among other countries, would clearly be ranked differently today.

What I've done in Chart 3 is looked at the period of disinflation: 1980–1993. It seems to me that around 1980 the countries of the industrialized world looked back at the 1970s and said: "Enough—indeed, too much. We had an awful lot of inflation, it didn't do anybody any good, and we ought to get rid of it." There was a kind of sea change in attitudes around the world, although not with exactly the same timing everywhere.

So Chart 3 examines the period between 1980 and 1993. Central banks are ranked by the objective index created by Cukierman *et al.*, with 1.0 connoting the most single-minded concentration on inflation reduction—you see, for example, that the Bundesbank is on the far right on this criterion— and with zero on the other extreme: banks that did not have any inflation objective at all in their charge (that includes the Bank of Japan and it included then, but not now, the Bank of France). And the question I asked was: Did the bank's legally stated objective make any difference to what happened in this 13-year period? Was there any systematic difference between the banks that were focused on inflation reduction and those that were not?

Well, the top panel shows the changes in inflation over that period. You can see that it is negative for every one of these countries; this was, after all, a period of disinflation. But the answer to the question is no. There is no correlation . . . between how much inflation fell and the legal charge of the central bank.

The lower panel shows that there was some correlation—not overwhelming, but noticeable—between the rise in unemployment and the central bank's objective. . . . So unemployment rose in every one of these countries, essentially; and it rose more in the countries whose central banks were more singlemindedly devoted to inflation reduction. But the difference is not tremendously significant. The message, I think, may be that the significance of the central bank's charge may be more apparent than real. But I wouldn't dismiss it entirely. Now, there is a two-handed answer for you!

CHART 3   Central Bank Objectives, Inflation, and Unemployment

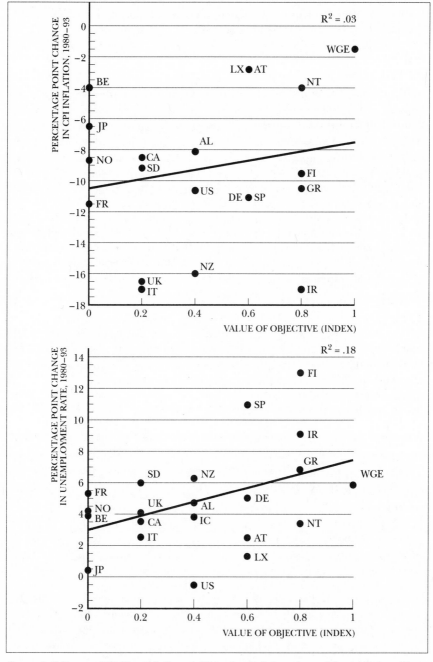

Source: A. Cukierman, S. Webb, and B. Neyapti, "Measuring the Independence of Central Banks and Its Effect on Policy Outcomes," *World Bank Economic Review* 6, 3 (September 1992) 353–398.

QUESTIONS FOR ANALYSIS

1. Why all the fuss about the money supply? What problems arise if the money supply grows too slowly? What problems arise if it grows too fast?

2. What is the money supply? Both Dr. Greenspan and Mr. Gonzalez refer to M2. What is M2?

3. Dr. Greenspan testified that: "The historical relationships between money and income, and between money and the price level, have largely broken down, depriving the aggregates of much of their usefulness as guides to policy. At least for the time being, M2 has been downgraded as a reliable indicator of financial conditions in the economy, and no single variable has yet been identified to take its place." How then can the Federal Reserve conduct monetary policy? If you were a member of the Federal Open Market Committee, how would you figure out whether money and credit should be tightened or loosened?

4. Mr. Gonzalez protests the Federal Reserve's lowering of the targets for money growth from 2 to 6 percent to 1 to 5 percent. In his view, "The money supply (defined as M2) should be growing at least as fast as the production of goods and services in a full employment economy." Why do you think that he believes this to be true? Do you agree? Why or why not?

5. Dr. Greenspan, concerned about inflationary pressures, says: "I believe we are on our way toward reestablishing the trust in the purchasing power of the dollar that is crucial to maximizing and fulfilling the productivity capacity of this nation." Why does he feel that it is so important to reestablish the trust in the purchasing power of the dollar? Do you agree with him? Why or why not?

6. In Dr. Greenspan's view, inflationary expectations have not been quelled. "Survey responses and financial market prices embody expectations that the current lower level of inflation not only will not be bettered, it will not even persist." Why is he so concerned about expectations? Isn't reality what is important, not expectations? How can the economy be hurt or threatened by something as ephemeral and hard-to-measure as expectations?

7. The real interest rate equals the interest rate minus the inflation rate. Dr. Greenspan says that short-term real interest rates, the interest rates "most directly affected by the Federal Reserve, are not far from zero." Why is the real interest rate of importance to policy makers? If the real interest rate is zero, does this indicate that money is easy or tight? Why?

8. According to Mr. Gonzalez, "With the economy stagnating as it is, a small increase in the money supply is not enough to reignite inflation." In what respects was the economy "stagnating" in July 1993? Contrast Mr. Gonzalez's views of the state of the economy and the likelihood of serious inflation with those of Mr. Greenspan.

9. In making decisions regarding monetary policy, must the Federal Reserve be concerned about the position and slope of the short-run aggregate supply curve? If so, why? If not, why not?

10. Mr. Gonzalez urged President Clinton "to consider changing the composition of the Federal Open Market Committee (FOMC) which decides our nation's monetary policies . . . [A]dvocates of price stability even at the price of stagnation are well-represented at the FOMC." Must we tolerate more inflation in order to reduce unemployment? Will inflation necessarily increase employment and output? Do you agree that the composition of the FOMC should be changed?

11. Subsequently, Alan Blinder of Princeton University, and Janet Yellen of the University of California at Berkeley, were appointed by President Clinton to the Federal Reserve Board. In late 1994, Dr. Blinder, vice-chairman of the board, made some remarks indicating that he would be less likely to increase interest rates when unemployment is high. An uproar resulted, after which he is reported to have said, "If you are on a central bank board, you ought to keep your mouth shut."* Do you agree with his original remarks? Why or why not? Do you agree that he ought to keep his mouth shut? Why or why not?

12. In late October, data issued by the U.S. Department of Commerce indicated that, in the third quarter of 1994, GDP grew at an annual rate of 3.4 percent, well in excess of the 2.5 percent growth rate that many people regarded as the maximum that could occur without causing increased inflation. On November 15, the Federal Open Market Committee raised the discount rate by 3/4 percentage point. Why?

13. What does Dr. Blinder have in mind when he says that "the effects of aggregate demand on jobs are temporary"?

14. Do you agree with Dr. Blinder that "the significance of the central bank's charge may be more apparent than real"? Why or why not?

*New York Times, September 11, 1994, p. 2F.

PART ELEVEN

INTER-
NATIONAL
TRADE
POLICY

The mid-1990s have seen a great deal of controversy over U.S. trade policy. Some influential political leaders and industrialists feel strongly that we should engage in "managed trade"; others disagree—equally strongly. The first article is by Paul Krugman of Massachusetts Institute of Technology who argues that the alleged competitiveness problem of the United States is greatly exaggerated. The second article is by Robert A. Lutz, president of the Chrysler Corporation, who favors managed trade. The third article is by Robert T. Parry, president of the Federal Reserve Bank of San Francisco, who opposes managed trade.

The Fixation on Competitiveness*

PAUL KRUGMAN

In the movie *The Music Man,* Robert Preston plays a traveling salesman who specializes in selling musical instruments and uniforms for marching bands to small towns. To make his sale in River City, he needs to convince local leaders that they have a problem he can solve. And so he manages to turn the formerly innocuous pool hall into a symbol of gathering social danger, to which the answer is, of course, the healthy town spirit that only a properly equipped school band can provide.

Many policy entrepreneurs (and to be honest, not a few professors) play a similar game. They have a solution; now they have to convince the politicians and the public that there is an appropriate problem. Often they fail: despite his best efforts, Robert Bartley of *The Wall Street Journal* never managed to convince many people that monetary chaos looms unless we put America back on the gold standard. Sometimes, however, policy entrepreneurs and the politicians who make alliance with them are spectacularly successful at creating imagined problems to which their favorite policy prescriptions are the answer.

The imaginary problem that galvanized the supply-siders and Ronald Reagan was the danger of Big Government: a government that taxed people too much, then wasted the money on legions of useless bureaucrats and

*This is an excerpt from Paul Krugman, *Peddling Prosperity* (New York: W. W. Norton, 1994). Paul Krugman is professor of economics at Massachusetts Institute of Technology.

generous welfare handouts to the undeserving poor. Big Government is not, of course, wholly imaginary. Taxes *are* a significant burden on all of us, and there are indeed useless bureaucrats and undeserving welfare recipients. But as a diagnosis of what was wrong with the American economy, it was deeply misleading; and the myth of Big Government both distracted America from coming to grips with its real problems and created new difficulties.

The supply-siders have now retreated to their think tanks, though they still hope to return for revenge. For the time being, Big Government is no longer an effective slogan, and middle-class Americans are angrier at the undeserving rich than the undeserving poor. But the policy entrepreneurs now riding high have convinced many Americans that we have a new kind of trouble in River City: trouble with a capital "C" that stands for "Competitiveness."

The strategic traders have now sold the American public (and for the most part themselves, for only a few policy entrepreneurs are entirely cynical) on the idea that our most crucial economic problem is our struggle with other advanced nations for global markets. The subtitle of Lester Thurow's *Head to Head* is "The Coming Economic Battle Among Japan, Europe, and America"; the jacket entices readers by saying, "The most decisive war of the century is being waged right now . . . and we may have already decided to lose."

Unfortunately, the alleged competitive problem of the United States is as much a fantasy as Reagan's myth of wasteful Big Government. The United States has some real problems in international competition, just as it really has some unproductive bureaucrats and welfare cheats. But in the image it conveys of what's really wrong with the economy, Clinton's rhetoric is as far off as Reagan's.

Economic rhetoric based on the myth of international competition as war has some advantages. It is easier to mobilize voters to support painful policies like tax increases and cuts in popular programs by claiming that the goal is national security—and President Clinton did just that in his highly effective 1993 State of the Union address. But ultimately the rhetoric of competitiveness will be destructive, because it can all too easily lead both to bad policies and to a neglect of the real issues.

The rise of the strategic traders poses two main risks. One is that in their effort to win global markets, they will destroy them instead. The other is that the commitment to a foolish ideology in one area will undermine economic policy across the board.

THE RISK OF TRADE WAR

There are two kinds of trade war: the imaginary ones that protectionists and strategic traders claim we are fighting all the time, and the real ones that happen when they get their way.

The fantasy of the strategic traders is that international trade is by its nature international competition—that countries that trade with each other are in a struggle over who gets the spoils. In reality there is almost nothing to this view: what a country gets depends almost entirely on its own performance, and there is nothing competitive about it. But when countries *believe* that they are in a competitive struggle, or when they become captive to the special interests that benefit from trade conflict, they can fall into what is generally known as a trade war.

A trade war in which countries restrict each other's exports in pursuit of some illusory advantage is not much like a real war. On one hand, nobody gets killed. On the other, unlike real wars, it is almost impossible for anyone to win, since the main losers when a country imposes barriers to trade are not foreign exporters but domestic residents. In effect, a trade war is a conflict in which each country uses most of its ammunition to shoot itself in the foot.

And yet once a trade war is started, it can be very difficult to stop. Each country finds it politically impossible to free up its trade without corresponding "concessions" from other countries, and these may be very hard to negotiate. In other words, once the world has gotten caught up in a wave of tit-for-tat protectionism, it can take decades to undo the damage.

Consider the lessons of the interwar period. A trade war among the advanced countries erupted after the United States passed the infamous Smoot-Hawley tariff in 1929, and intensified as countries made desperate efforts to find ways out of the Great Depression. Yet most people, even including the senators who voted for Smoot-Hawley, soon realized that protectionism had gone too far. The United States began trying to negotiate tariffs down again as early as 1934, and after World War II both the political and the economic environment were very favorable for trade liberalization. Once the global trading system had been shattered, however, it was very hard to put back together; trade among industrial countries didn't regain its 1914 level until 1970.

In the 1990s, the world is ripe for another outbreak of trade war. The key economic ingredients that led to protectionism in the interwar period—slow growth, persistent high unemployment—are back again, especially in Europe. Meanwhile, the political strengths that helped make the freeing up of trade after World War II possible—a strong leading nation and a common purpose—are gone with the relative decline of the United States and the end of the Cold War. It wouldn't take much miscalculation to start a round of tariffs, countertariffs, and mutual recrimination that could repeat the interwar experience of shrinking trade.

Would this be a catastrophe? No, but it would add significantly to our problems. Big, largely self-contained economies like the United States, the European Community, and Japan could take restricted global trade in stride. Even a quite nasty trade war would reduce their real income only a percentage point or two. But smaller countries, more dependent on world markets to help them make up for the small size of their internal markets and their limited resources, would either have to scramble to form commercial alliances with the big players or be left dangerously out in the cold. It would not be surprising if a world of trade conflict among the big advanced countries was a world of political instability, and maybe growing anti-Western feeling, in smaller and poorer countries from Latin America to the former Soviet Republics.

World trade, then, is in an endangered state, in which we could easily stumble into an era of trade conflict that would be at least as hard to get rid of as Ronald Reagan's deficit. Yet it is at this of all moments that strategic traders in the United States think that we need to get tough with other countries in pursuit of "competitiveness."

Imagine the following scenario: Clinton administration officials—ignoring advice from conventional economists—decide that Japan's trade surplus is the root of many of America's economic difficulties, and decide to demand that Japan not only take measures to reduce that surplus but agree to meet specific numerical targets. The Japanese are indignant: they point out, correctly, that it is perfectly reasonable for a country with a very high savings rate to invest a significant fraction of those savings abroad, and that Japan's trade surplus is simply the other side of its capital account deficit. Besides, they say, what are they supposed to do—run huge budget deficits to soak up all that private saving?

The strategic traders in the Clinton administration nonetheless present their demands at an economic summit—and the Japanese reject them. At this point the U.S. government faces a dilemma. To drop the issue would look like weakness; but there is no real policy option other than to close U.S. markets to Japanese goods. And so protectionism it is—a protectionism that is matched by Japanese retaliation and European emulation. Within two years the results of four decades of negotiations to open world markets are reversed.

An unlikely scenario? At the time of writing, much of it had already happened. The Treasury Department is usually a bastion of free trade thinking, but in May 1993 Lawrence Summers, now the Undersecretary of the Treasury for International Affairs, asserted in a speech that "Japan's surplus is the major asymmetry in the global economy" and that this surplus was a "significant drag on global growth"; he followed this assertion with the statement that "The United States will focus less on process and more on results, and results have to be measurable." Everyone knew what he meant: the U.S. Trade Representative had for several weeks been telling reporters that the United States was likely to demand that Japan impose a ceiling on its trade surplus at the next meeting of the Group of Seven industrial countries. Meanwhile, Japanese officials and the Japanese public were furious and defiant in the face of American pressure.

One hopes that by the time this book is published this particular scenario will turn out to have been a premature alarm. As long as the administration is committed to the ideology of strategic trade, however, the risk of trade war will remain high.

So the direct threat from the ascendancy of strategic traders is that their fixation on the supposed problem of competitiveness will set off a trade war. Like the budget deficit created by the supply-siders, a trade war will not destroy the U.S. economy; but also like the budget deficit, it will be very hard to get rid of.

Managed Trade*

ROBERT A. LUTZ

Thank you, Dean Hasler. And good morning to all of you. It's great to be back here at my alma mater. I have a lot of fond memories of Berkeley, starting with the fact that I got a terrific education here from an absolutely brilliant faculty.

I also remember that going to school here—back in those, the earliest days of the Free Speech Movement—was a real lesson in *character-building* for me. You see, I'd already been in the Marine Corps before I started school, and, while in school, I continued as a First Lieutenant in the reserves.

And, since I had a crew cut, an affinity for the military, and wrote letters to the "Daily Californian," I sort of became the resident right-wing speaker at a host of panel discussions around campus. The Free-Speech types didn't want to appear biased, so they put this obviously wacko, lunatic-fringe conservative on their panels just to sort of even things out.

The funny thing, however, is that I was actually a *moderate!* I just *looked* conservative by comparison!

And I must say, it's good to see that things haven't changed much here. I read recently about how you had a student who was coming to class in the nude—"The Naked Guy," I believe he was called? I especially liked it when,

*This speech was delivered at the Haas School of Business Faculty–Alumni Colloquium, University of California at Berkeley, on April 24, 1993. Robert A. Lutz is president of the Chrysler Corporation.

after he got expelled, he said, "My original plan was that I was going to get expelled and then sue for readmittance. *I can learn a lot suing them.*"

Now, I've heard of "independent study," but I think that's a little *ridiculous*—even for Berkeley!

Anyway, it's great to be back here. And I'd like to begin by commending you for choosing a quote-unquote "global focus" for your discussions here at this colloquium today. It's become a cliche, of course, but the business world today truly *is* a global world.

And we in the auto business perhaps know that better than most. Ever since the two oil shocks of the 1970s gave foreign automakers (most notably the Japanese) their first real toehold in this market, we in Detroit have had to struggle with the realities of tough international competition coming at us each and every day right here in our own back yard.

And, though it wasn't always easy, we've learned a lot from that experience.

We've learned, for instance, that over time there's been a certain convergence in consumer tastes around the world. No longer do you have the stereotype of Americans driving nothing but land yachts, Japanese driving nothing but minicars, and Europeans driving spartan econocars. Today, cars like, say, the Honda Accord, the Ford Taurus, or like my company's new Chrysler Concorde, Dodge Intrepid, and Eagle Vision sedans fit in virtually anywhere in the world.

We've also learned that you can run, but you can't hide, when it comes to dealing with international competition. In fact, I daresay that any company today that is still benchmarking just—or even *primarily*—its domestic competitors is probably doomed to failure.

And finally, we've learned that nothing is forever—that, with hard work, even the most seemingly permanent of trends can indeed be turned around. Case in point: In the past 15 months, Chrysler has gained more than two points of total market share in the U.S. And in that same period, the Japanese automakers as a whole have *lost* five-and-a-half points of share. That, I submit, is a *sea change* if there ever was one!

But for all that globalization and international competition has taught us in recent years, we have also learned that global trade has a dark side—a *very* dark side. And that dark side is that not all countries in the world play by the same rules when it comes to international trade.

Oh, sure, everybody pays homage to the GATT, and everybody professes to be "free traders." But, in reality, most everybody in the world—with the notable exception of the United States—practices something that has come to be known as "*managed* trade."

And that's a fact, I know, that the head of President Clinton's Council of Economic Advisers, Berkeley's own Laura D'Andrea Tyson, has herself pointed out many times. The term I believe she likes to use is "aggressive unilateralism." That is, the United States shouldn't be afraid to act *aggressively* and *unilaterally* (if need be) in demanding trade agreements that would, in fact, help *increase* world trade. In other words, in the face of managed trade, we shouldn't be afraid to practice a little managed trade ourselves.

Now, I know that Professor Tyson and others in the Clinton Administration have taken a lot of heat for their views. For example, in the *New York Times* last month, Jagdish Bhagwati of Columbia University said, "This should be the spring of hope, and instead we might get nuclear winter."

Which brings me to the (I hope) rather catchy title of my talk here today: "Managed Trade: Spring of Hope or Nuclear Winter?" In other words: Should managed trade be a part of this country's economic strategy in the context of today's global economy—part of, if you will, our "spring of hope," especially as we strive for some long-overdue economic revitalization?

Or is it, as Professor Bhagwati suggests, a step down a slippery slope leading to a 1930s-style trade war and to a sort of economic nuclear winter?

That's the central question that I'd like to address here today. And by way of illustration, I'd like to use some examples from the auto industry—not just because I know it best, but because the auto industry—the good ol' "smokestack," "sunset" auto industry—is shaping up to be one of *the* prime battlegrounds for global trade issues today. As President Clinton's Trade Representative, Mickey Kantor, put it recently, Detroit is at "the *nerve center* of America's new trade and economic dialogue."

Why? Well, because autos and auto parts have accounted for more than *two-thirds* of America's absolutely staggering $450-*billion*-dollar trade deficit with Japan over the past decade. Obviously, therefore, our *overall* trade deficit cannot come down unless the *auto* deficit is attacked.

Let me tell a story that's been very much in the news lately and which, I think, pretty well symbolizes our whole auto trade with Japan. It's the story of multipurpose vehicles, or "MPVs" for short. An MPV is a vehicle like, say, the Toyota 4-Runner sport utility.

A funny thing happens to a 4-Runner when it's imported into this country. Four U.S. regulators all look it over. The fellow from the Environmental Protection Agency inspects it and declares that it is "a truck," and will therefore only have to meet the emissions standards for U.S. trucks, which are not as strict as those for cars.

Behind him is the man from the National Highway Traffic Safety Administration, who certifies that it is indeed a truck so it won't have to have the same safety devices as a car.

And then comes the inspector from the Department of Transportation, who also agrees that the vehicle is a truck so it won't have to meet the higher fuel economy requirements of a car.

But then comes the fourth inspector. He's from the U.S. Customs Service. He looks at the 4-Runner and says, "Nope, this isn't a truck at all; it's a *car!*" And that means it pays a duty of only 2.5 percent instead of the 25 percent duty on trucks.

Now, what's going on here? Well, back in February of 1989, after intense lobbying by Japanese automakers, the U.S. Treasury Department, in a virtually unprecedented decision, overruled its own Customs Service and reclassified Japanese sport utilities and minivans from trucks to cars. It was, as President Clinton himself put it in a press conference last month, a "$300-million-dollar-a-year freebie to the Japanese for no apparent reason."

Now, maybe it wouldn't have been so bad if the U.S. had gotten some trade concessions *of its own* in return. But we got absolutely *nothing*. Now, I daresay that if a business student here at the Haas School suggested such an obviously win-*lose* deal as a solution to a case study, he'd be joining "The Naked Guy" out on the street!

But that's not the only trade issue related to autos that's been in the news lately. The other one is *dumping*.

As you may know, earlier this year General Motors, Ford, and Chrysler had contemplated filing a dumping charge against Japanese automakers. We had, quite frankly, what we considered to be a *very* strong case. (And it applied, by the way, to *all* major Japanese automakers, across *all* segments of the market—from small cars to luxury cars. And we're talking about cars being dumped for as much as *$5,000* below their prices in Japan. So, this was no inconsequential matter.)

But we backed off—at least for now—in part to give the Clinton Administration a chance to try to solve the problem, and in part, again quite frankly, because of the well-orchestrated negative PR campaign that we were already beginning to experience for even *thinking* about filing a charge.

Now, in concert with that high-priced PR campaign, the Japanese automakers, of course, swore up and down that they were *not* dumping. However, they've nonetheless quietly been raising their prices in recent months (even *before* the yen started to rise)—which might, I think, lead a cynic to believe that just maybe they'd rather pocket the money themselves than have the U.S. government get it in added tariffs!

Meanwhile, amid all the PR and all of the mud-slinging, a couple of simple things seemed to have gotten lost: One is that dumping is *against the law*—against both U.S. *and* international trade law. And Japan certainly knows that as well as anybody, given that they just recently imposed anti-dumping duties of *their own*—on manganese coming in from China!

The other thing that seems to have gotten lost is that "managed trade" is really *already* being practiced here in the United States—only it's all too often the *Japanese,* and not us, who are managing it!

Now, at this point, I know that perhaps some of you might be inclined to say, "Hey, why don't you guys in Detroit quit whining, and just shut up and compete?"

Well, we *are* competing. Earlier, I mentioned the market share that we at Chrysler have won back here in the U.S. We've also, by the way, been doing quite well in Europe. From a virtual standstill, we've sold more than 200,000 vehicles in Europe in the last four years. And so far *this* year, our European sales are *up* 30 percent, while the market as a whole is *down* 17 percent.

But the one place where we continue to have very little success at all is— you guessed it—*Japan.*

And it's not just us—*no* foreign automakers really have had any success to speak of in Japan. In fact, total import penetration in the Japanese auto market was less than *three* percent last year. By contrast, the Japanese have routinely taken up to *ten times* that amount of the U.S. market (and here in California, of course, it's been more like *15* times).

Now, why is that? Well, let me cite the case of Chrysler's new Jeep Grand Cherokee sport utility (which, by the way, competes head to head with the Toyota 4-Runner). The Grand Cherokee is, by any measure, a world-class vehicle. It won Motor Trend's "Truck of the Year" award last year. And it's completely sold out both here in the United States and in Europe.

Yet we have a tough time selling Grand Cherokees *in Japan.* And no wonder, given that they cost over $15,000 *more* in Japan than they do here!

That's because the Japanese won't accept our certifications, because everything has to be inspected, and mostly because of the maze of red tape and gargantuan distribution costs associated with Japan's notoriously closed distribution system.

And "closed" it is. In fact, until just recently, Japanese automakers prevented their dealers in Japan from selling any imported cars at all!

Now, if we did this in the U.S., of course, we'd be thrown in jail for violating antitrust laws. But in Japan, it's been standard practice. And, as a result, while foreign cars are sold today at more than *90* percent of all dealerships in the United States, foreign cars are sold at just *seven* percent of all dealerships in Japan!

But, of course, it's not just cars that have been kept out of Japan. The list of products is, in my view, embarrassingly long. And, of course, as the folks down in Silicon Valley know all too well, that list includes *computer chips.*

Now, I understand that trade tensions eased a bit out here recently when it was announced that, in the fourth quarter, U.S. and other foreign semiconductor makers had finally—*finally*—achieved the target of 20 percent of the Japanese chip market. But I think it's worth keeping in mind *how* our chip makers actually achieved that goal.

The process began way back in 1985, when the Reagan Administration (of all people!) accepted an anti-dumping case and a "Super 301" unfair trade case brought against the Japanese. That "chip shot," as it was called, then eventually led to negotiations, which, in turn, produced the 20-percent import target. (And I understand, by the way, that that 20-percent figure is still less than *half* the market share that U.S. chip makers enjoy *elsewhere* in the world. And it's also almost identical to the share of the *U.S.* chip market that *Japanese* companies enjoy!)

Anyway, the upshot is that in the case of computer chips the U.S. followed a policy of, yes, *managed trade.* In fact, it was one that definitely contained some Laura Tyson-style "aggressive unilateralism." And, lo and behold, it's *working*!

Now, I know that Professor Tyson along with others in the Administration, such as Mickey Kantor, have been called "trade agnostics" for their pragmatic, results-oriented approach to global trade. And I'm sure those who say that often mean it in a derogatory sense—that Tyson and Kantor and others have somehow lost their ideological souls.

But I, for one, think there's a big difference between being a trade *atheist* (that is, somebody who *has* lost his soul and given up on free trade altogether) and a trade *agnostic.* A trade agnostic, it seems to me, is someone who believes that real free trade could indeed exist in the world someday— but who in the meantime speaks softly and carries a big stick!

By that definition, the *Europeans,* to name just one example, are certainly trade agnostics. Last year—as part of the "EC '92" negotiations—the European Community told Japanese automakers that they can have no more than *16 percent* of the European auto market through the end of this century. (That compares, despite their recent losses, to the *24*-percent share of the market that the Japanese have in the *U.S.* today.)

Now, I know that Professor Tyson herself might even say that an industry like autos is too mature, and too "low-tech," to qualify for the benefits of managed trade here in this country.

But, for starters, we're hardly low-tech. You may not know this, but the auto industry buys *20 percent*—that's *one in five*—of all the semiconductors sold in this country. In fact, a car today with an air bag, ABS brakes, and traction control has the computing power of the on-board guidance system of the Apollo moonshot!

(And, by the way, I think that Silicon Valley should be more than a little dismayed by reports recently that while U.S. chip makers supply *60* percent of the chips that go into luxury cars worldwide—the kind of cars most likely *to have* traction control and that other high-tech stuff—their market share of the Japanese luxury brands Lexus and Infiniti is just *seven* percent!)

And as far as being a so-called "mature" industry goes—yes, the auto industry is guilty of being mature. But the fact is, every industry in this country *aspires* to be mature one day. We *all* want to perpetuate ourselves. But think about this: If we allow *today's* high-employment, high-value-added, mature industries to become victims of *somebody else's* managed-trade policies, than what does that bode for the mature industries of *tomorrow?*

Going back to Europe, the Europeans have basically said that their key, strategic industries, including autos, and the jobs that they represent are *important* to them. Now, maybe in the case of Airbus and agricultural subsidies, they've gone overboard a little bit! But by and large, they have, in my opinion, found a much better trade-off than we have between the so-called "rights of the consumer" and *also*-very-legitimate rights of those very same citizens to be gainfully employed.

Which makes sense. After all, if you think about it, the most useless consumer of all is one *without a job!*

For some reason, we haven't seemed quite ready to grasp that reality here in this country. Although in this so-called "jobless recovery" of ours, and with all of the so-called "hollowing-out" of American industry that's taken place over the last decade or so (including the layoffs at IBM and elsewhere in high tech), I think maybe we're *beginning* to understand.

And I also think that we're finally beginning to understand that our trade policies (or lack thereof) have definitely played a *key role* in that hollowing-out and in that joblessness.

So, to get back to my central question—"Managed Trade: Spring of Hope or Nuclear Winter?"—I think, in truth, that we are actually experiencing a bit of "nuclear winter" *right now!* (Or maybe you might call it *"neutron* winter"—the buildings are still standing, it's just the *jobs* that are gone!)

I also think that if we want to get this economy moving strongly forward again, and *keep* it moving forward as a global leader into the 21st century, then there's no doubt that a more pragmatic—indeed, one might say a more *realistic*—trade policy needs to be adopted. *That,* in my opinion, is our "spring of hope."

And if that sounds like "trade agnosticism," then so be it. But in my book, it makes a whole lot more sense to be an agnostic on this subject than a so-called "true believer" who keeps waiting for his savior . . . but in the meantime winds up getting crucified *himself!*

And on that note, I'd like to thank you for letting this "prodigal-son-of-Berkeley-turned-trade-agnostic" return to his alma mater to offer his I-hope-not-*too*-blasphemous opinions.

If nothing else, it's nice knowing, all these years later, that I'm probably no longer the resident conservative here on campus!

Thank you very much.

U.S. Trade Deficits and International Competitiveness*

ROBERT T. PARRY

hank you. It's a pleasure to be here. Today I'd like to talk about our trade deficit and what it implies about our ability to compete globally. We've had this trade deficit for over a decade. Some people, and a number of policymakers, see this as a symptom that we've lost our edge in international competition. Here's their diagnosis of the problem: Foreign competitors are able to take markets away from U.S. producers because they have some important advantages. In particular, they have lower wages, superior technology, and "unfair" trade practices.

What's their prescription to fix the problem and return U.S. industries to competitive health? They'd like to see the government try to manage international competition by taking a more protectionist stance and targeting certain industries for special support.

My own view is that this analysis is off the mark. I do *not* think the trade deficit is due to lower wages, superior technology, and "unfair" trade practices abroad. On the contrary, I think we can find the sources of the trade deficit in certain macroeconomic fundamentals—namely, our own government budget deficit and our investment and saving patterns. Moreover, I don't think the trade deficit is necessarily the best way to judge our com-

*This speech was delivered to the National Association of Business Economists in Chicago, Illinois, on September 20, 1993. Robert T. Parry is president of the Federal Reserve Bank of San Francisco.

petitiveness. There are more important factors to consider. In particular, I would point to price competitiveness and productivity.

Let me begin by looking at just how bad the trade deficit is. First, I think it's a mistake to focus too much on the most recent numbers, which haven't been too good. The reason it's a mistake is that the source of the problem is more cyclical than it is structural. The U.S. has been in recovery for a while now. But many of our industrial trading partners are still in recession. So the recent bulge in our trade deficit is largely due to the fact that, as we continue to grow and import more, the weakness abroad is hurting our exports.

Now let me look at the longer view. Although the trade deficit has persisted for over a decade, the situation is much better now than it was in the mid-1980s. The merchandise trade deficit fell from a peak of $160 billion in 1987 to $96 billion in 1992. Relative to GDP, it declined from 3.5 percent to 1.6 percent. The current account deficit, which includes trade in services, improved even more dramatically. It dropped from a deficit of $167 billion in 1987 to $62 billion in 1992—or from 3.5 percent of GDP to 1 percent of GDP.

Why the turnaround? Because over the past six years, U.S. exports have surged. From 1986 through 1992 the total value of U.S. merchandise exports almost doubled, growing more than 12 percent per year. In volume terms, exports grew almost as fast, averaging more than 10 percent per year. A major source of strength in this export growth has been manufactures. And it's notable that this sector has continued to show strength even during the worldwide economic slowdown of the past few years. So the big picture on the trade deficit is that the situation is better than it was in the mid-1980s, because U.S. exports have surged since then.

Now let me look at the problem of "unfair trade practices." By this I mean such things as government support of selected industries through export subsidies and trade protection. The evidence is clear that virtually all countries, including the U.S., impose at least some restrictions on imports and provide government support for exports. Still, there's *no* evidence that the U.S. trade deficits of the 1980s were caused by greater foreign trade barriers or other unfair trade practices. First of all, between 1981 and 1987, when the deficit was at its peak, the deterioration in our trade position was *pervasive.* It spread uniformly and proportionately across capital goods, automotive products, and consumer goods. And the deterioration was roughly in proportion to each of our major trading partner's share of U.S. import and exports in 1981. If unfair foreign trade practices had caused the pervasive decline in the early 1980s, they would have had to change uniformly and suddenly around 1981, an unlikely conspiracy.

Of all the U.S. trading partners, Japan continues to be singled out for having the most unfair trading practices. But it's doubtful that such policies have been a major cause of U.S. trade deficits. First of all, the Japanese market has become somewhat more *open*—not more closed—over the past decade. Second, Japan's share of changes in the total U.S. non-oil merchandise trade deficit have been proportional to its U.S. trade share. For example, in 1981, about 9 percent of our exports went to Japan, and about 20 percent of our imports came from Japan. That left us with a bilateral deficit of $16 billion. If the same shares prevailed in 1992, we would have had a bilateral deficit of $57 billion—which is in fact a little larger than the actual deficit of $51 billion. So I think there's not much evidence to say that restrictive trade practices have been the driving force behind changes in the U.S. trade deficit.

Of course, the doors to Japanese and other foreign markets aren't exactly wide open to U.S. exporters. But even if existing foreign restrictions on U.S. exports were completely removed, most estimates suggest we'd reduce our trade deficit by only modest amounts.

Now let me look at our international competitiveness in terms of our production costs and productivity. Is there any evidence that U.S. price competitiveness declined during the 1980s? If we make the comparison in dollar terms, then the answer is: "Yes, price competitiveness *did* decline." Between 1980 and 1985 unit labor costs in dollars rose at an annual rate of 3.1 percent in the U.S., while unit labor costs fell in 10 of 11 other industrial countries.

But that information doesn't give us a complete picture. If we make the comparison in national currency terms, then unit labor costs actually *rose* in most of those other countries. Therefore, it was the appreciation of the dollar in the early 1980s, not underlying cost increases, that primarily caused U.S. manufacturers to lose price competitiveness to foreign producers during this period.

The fall of the dollar since the mid-1980s has made foreign unit labor costs measured in dollars now substantially higher than they were in 1980. Between the 1985 peak in the dollar and 1992, U.S. unit labor costs rose at only 1 percent per year, while costs in Japan, France, Germany, Korea, and Taiwan, for example, all rose at roughly 10 percent annually over the period 1985–1992. Therefore, most of the apparent improvement in U.S. international competitiveness is due to changes in the value of the dollar. Furthermore, manufacturing in the U.S. now appears to have a significant cost advantage over manufacturing in other countries.

What about productivity? The U.S. had relatively *strong* productivity growth during the 1980s. Between 1980 and 1985, manufacturers' output per worker grew 3.3 percent annually in the U.S., compared to 4.0 percent in Japan, 2.3 percent in France, and 2.1 percent in Germany. Since the mid-1980s U.S. productivity has continued to keep pace and even exceed that in much of the rest of the world. From 1985 to 1992 U.S. manufacturing output per worker grew at 2.9 percent per year, compared to 2.3 percent in Japan, 0.8 percent in Germany, and 2.8 percent in France.

Now that we can't blame the trade deficit on our competitors' lower labor costs, higher productivity, or unfair trade practices, where do we look for the source of it? The answer, I think, is in macroeconomic fundamentals. By definition, a country's trade balance is the mirror image of its pattern of saving and investment. So, for example, a country with more investment opportunities than its domestic saving can handle will borrow from abroad and run a trade deficit. This is true even if its costs are relatively low, its home markets are protected, and its exports are subsidized. The converse also holds true: A country with high saving relative to investment will run trade *surpluses*—even if its markets are open and its products are regarded as "noncompetitive."

In the case of the U.S., the emergence and persistence of large trade deficits since the early 1980s can be attributed largely to changes in the nation's saving-investment balance. Over the 1960s and 1970s, the U.S. (gross) national saving rate roughly equaled the investment rate and remained constant at about 20 percent of GNP. As a result the current account remained approximately in balance. But in the early 1980s, the national saving rate fell, largely because of bigger government budget deficits. The resulting net saving deficit led to higher real interest rates, the appreciation of the dollar, and the associated current account deficits that emerged in the early 1980s. In the second half of the 1980s the budget deficit turned around somewhat, interest rates and the dollar fell, and the current account deficit began to narrow.

So it's primarily *macroeconomic developments* that explain the worsening of the U.S. trade balance in the early 1980s followed by its improvement later in the decade. To keep the trend of improvement going in the long run, we'll need further macroeconomic policy adjustments. Ideally, we'd accomplish this through either a fiscal contraction or an increase in private saving. Less ideally, we could accomplish it through a reduction in domestic investment. The current plans for reduced federal budget deficits are in the right direction.

In conclusion, I think the U.S. is in reasonably good competitive shape. U.S. exports have boomed and the trade deficit is lower than it was in the mid-1980s. More important, measures of labor costs and productivity, particularly in manufacturing, indicate resurgent U.S. price competitiveness. U.S. productivity growth in the 1980s has been comparable with and, in some cases better than, other industrial countries abroad. The continued existence of U.S. trade deficits reflects an imbalance of national saving below investment, not any fundamental decline in U.S. international competitiveness.

Of course, when you talk about competition, you're always talking about winners and losers. And there's no question that some industries are going to continue to face difficult times from foreign competitors. But the real winners will be consumers for whom foreign competition means better quality U.S. products. The experience of the U.S. automobile industry is a case in point. Moreover, in a dynamic competitive world economy, with new products, technologies, and production processes continually becoming available, there will always be some firms on the decline as others are on the rise. The appropriate policy response to an industry that's losing ground to foreign competition is not to erect barriers to imports, but rather to facilitate the redirection of workers who lose jobs to more productive employment opportunities elsewhere. If the protectionist route is followed, newer, more efficient industries will have less scope to expand, and overall output and economic welfare will suffer.

And this brings me back to the main question of this conference: U.S. prosperity in a competitive world. The real issue of our long-term prosperity, of maintaining and improving American living standards, doesn't depend on how stiff the competition is abroad. It depends primarily on our *own* productivity growth and our ability to maintain a stable economic environment. The Federal Reserve has a role in this, of course. And that is to conduct a low-inflation monetary policy. But that's not enough. This country also must grapple with the hard issues of devising the means to boost productivity—

☐ with policies that foster greater private capital formation,

☐ with policies that increase investment in infrastructure,

☐ with policies that expand research and development expenditures,

☐ with policies that improve the quality of education,

☐ and with policies that stimulate entrepreneurial activity.

To sum this all up: Our prosperity doesn't depend on distorting markets with industrial policies and protectionist barriers; instead it depends on improving our productivity and letting markets work to bring out the best in our natural and human resources.

Thank you.

QUESTIONS FOR ANALYSIS

1. Professor Krugman seems to fear that a trade war may break out between the United States and Japan. Why?

2. If a trade war were to break out, would it matter? Why or why not?

3. If the United States has a comparative advantage in the production of pharmaceuticals and if Japan has a comparative advantage in the production of autos, what are the advantages in the U.S.'s specialization in pharmaceuticals and Japan's specialization in autos?

4. If the United States has a comparative advantage in the production of pharmaceuticals, can we be sure that the United States will be an exporter of pharmaceuticals? Why or why not?

5. Mr. Lutz states that: "Last year . . . the European Community told Japanese automakers that they can have no more than *16 percent* of the European auto market through the end of this century." What groups gain from this policy, and why? What groups lose from this policy, and why?

6. Mr. Lutz goes on to say that "the Europeans have basically said that their key, strategic industries, including autos, and the jobs that they represent are *important* to them . . . [B]y and large, they have, in my opinion, found a much better trade-off than we have between the so-called 'rights of the consumer' and *also*-very-legitimate rights of those very same citizens to be gainfully employed." Why does Mr. Lutz believe such a tradeoff exists? Do you agree? Why or why not?

7. According to Mr. Lutz, "earlier this year General Motors, Ford, and Chrysler had contemplated filing a dumping charge against Japanese automakers . . . (And we're talking about cars being dumped for as much as $5,000 below their prices in Japan. So, this was no inconsequential matter.)" What is wrong with Japanese automakers selling their cars in the United States for $5,000 less than in Japan?

8. Mr. Parry does *"not* think that the trade deficit is due to lower wages, superior technology, and 'unfair' trade practices abroad. On the contrary, [he thinks] we can find the sources of the trade deficit in certain macroeconomic fundamentals—namely, our own government budget deficit and our investment and saving patterns." What has the government budget deficit got to do with our trade deficit? Is it true that our investment and saving patterns are related to our trade deficit? If so, explain in detail what the relationships are.

9. According to Mr. Parry, "I don't think the trade deficit is necessarily the best way to judge our competitiveness. There are more important factors to consider.

In particular, I would point to price competitiveness and productivity." Why are these factors important in this regard?

10. Mr. Parry concludes that: "Our prosperity doesn't depend on distorting markets with industrial policies and protectionist barriers; instead it depends on improving our productivity and letting markets work to bring out the best in our natural and human resources." Do you agree? Why or why not?

11. Mr. Parry points out that productivity in manufacturing grew more rapidly during 1985–92 in the United States than in Japan, Germany, or France. Does this mean that productivity in the entire economy grew faster in the United States than in these other countries? What are the problems in measuring productivity in industries producing services? Will the rate of productivity growth be increased by policies that (a) increase private capital formation, (b) expand research and development expenditures, (c) improve the quality of education?

12. What can the federal government do to (a) increase private capital formation, (b) expand research and development, (c) improve the quality of education?